Social Studies Activities A to Z

Joanne Matricardi
Jeanne McLarty

THOMSON

DELMAR LEARNING

Australia   Brazil   Canada   Mexico   Singapore   Spain   United Kingdom   United States

THOMSON

DELMAR LEARNING

Social Studies Activities A to Z
Joanne Matricardi and Jeanne McLarty

Vice President, Career Education Strategic Business Unit:
Dawn Gerrain

Director of Learning Solutions:
John Fedor

Managing Editor:
Robert L. Serenka, Jr.

Senior Acquisitions Editor:
Erin O'Connor

Product Manager:
Philip Mandl

Editorial Assistant:
Alison Archambault

Director of Production:
Wendy A. Troeger

Production Manager:
Mark Bernard

Content Project Manager:
Karin Hillen Jaquays

Technology Project Manager:
Sandy Charette

Director of Marketing:
Wendy E. Mapstone

Channel Manager:
Kristin McNary

Marketing Coordinator:
Scott A. Chrysler

Marketing Specialist:
Erica S. Conley

Art Director:
Joy Kocsis

Cover Design:
Joseph Villanova

Any additional questions about permissions can be submitted by email to thomsonrights@thomson.com

Library of Congress Cataloging-in-Publication Data

Matricardi, Joanne.
  Social studies activities A to Z / Joanne Matricardi and Jeanne McLarty.
     p. cm.
  Includes bibliographical references and index.
  ISBN-13 978-1-4180-4848-8
  ISBN-10 1-4180-4848-8
  (alk. paper)
  1. Social sciences—Study and teaching (Early childhood)—Activity programs.
I. McLarty, Jeanne.   II. Title.
  LB1139.5.S64M38 2008
  372.83—dc22

                                          2007006537

NOTICE TO THE READER

Contents

Preface

Social Studies is a very broad topic. It is a curriculum area that permeates everything we do. It is our culture, communities, holidays, foods, customs, occupations, diversity, respect for others, and our emotional and social growth. A child's self-awareness can be fostered through a social studies curriculum as they come to appreciate their uniqueness yet sameness with others.

The purpose of *Social Studies Activities A to Z* is to provide teachers, parents, and student teachers with a collection of activities to promote awareness of these topics. The activities are used across the curriculum, integrating art, blocks, cooking, dramatic play, group time, language arts, manipulatives, math, outdoor play, science, and snack time. Some of them cross curriculum boundaries and may be used in multiple areas.

Social Studies Activities A to Z presents activities in an alphabetical layout. This allows adults to link the curriculum to a specific letter of the alphabet. Early childhood classrooms may have a letter of the week. This book provides an easy way for social studies activities to highlight a particular letter.

Some of the lessons offered include the use of patterns in the creation of materials. All suggested patterns are located in the Appendix. The patterns are not meant to use only one time. Materials should be carefully created and preserved for future service. The "Helpful Hints" section of this book contains suggestions for material preservation. Two additional appendixes contain sample family letters and a world map. Many activities in this text highlight different countries. The world map identifies the countries that are emphasized.

The activities are presented in a lesson plan format. There are six areas: "Developmental Goals," "Learning Objective," "Discussion Suggestions," "Materials," "Adult Preparation," and "Procedures." The developmental goals offer social-emotional, physical, and cognitive concepts to be explored. The learning objective states what the children will use to accomplish the immediate goal of the lesson. The discussion suggestions offer the adult background information about the activity and recommend information to talk about with the children. The materials section presents all that is required from the preparation through the implementation of the activity. The procedures section involves a step-by-step process for the child to successfully accomplish the lesson.

Additional sections may be included in the lesson plan format. At times notes are given for the activity. These notes point out special considerations for the adult.

Safety precautions are also presented when objects used by children may necessitate a need for closer supervision. Expansions may be offered for some activities. This is a way to extend the lesson. Book suggestions are given for the majority of the activities. Always review a book before using it with the children. Some of them may not be suitable for all children. If a book appears too long, it is appropriate to paraphrase the text to accommodate shorter attention spans.

Age appropriateness for each activity is given. This is just a suggestion. Knowing the children's abilities and attention span will help determine what activities may be done and whether or not they need to be altered.

All of the activities in *Social Studies Activities A to Z* that focus on a different country offer the use of a globe to help children identify where they live and where the object country is in relation to their home. At first, the value of using a globe with preschoolers may appear too abstract. However, using this technique each time another country is discussed will help children build a context of knowledge.

Some holiday activities are included in this book. Some people may be concerned about using religious or ethnically based activities. One of the purposes of social studies is to value other cultures. We live in a diverse society. Helping others celebrate their culture shows an appreciation of our differences.

Social Studies Activities A to Z provides a "Curriculum Index." This allows the adult to select activities to emphasize a particular center. However you choose to implement the use of these activities in your classroom or home is left to your discretion.

An online resource (http://www.earlychilded.delmar.com) is an accompaniment to *Social Studies Activities A to Z.* This site contains additional group activities for young children. The activities are written in the same lesson plan format found in this book. These detailed plans include developmental goals, learning objectives, a list of materials, directions for adult preparation, and a step-by-step procedure for the child. The activities are easy to understand and implement, either in the preschool classroom or at home. The *Social Studies Activities A to Z* online resource also provides links to related preschool sites. These links contain additional ideas, patterns, book sources, and other social studies materials.

ACKNOWLEDGMENTS

This book is an accumulation of original and shared ideas developed over 45 years of teaching young children. Many thanks to our co-workers, students, and their parents for sharing and experimenting with us. We, and the editors at Thomson Delmar Learning, would also like to thank the following reviewers for their time, effort, and thoughtful contributions which helped to shape the final text:

Lynnette J. McCarty
President, NACCP
Owner, Serendipity Children's Center
Tumwater, Washington

Patricia Capistron
Lead Teacher
Rocking Unicorn Nursery School
West Chatham, Massachusetts

Meredith E. Chambers, M.Ed.
Language Literacy Specialist, Head Teacher
Chinese American Service League-Child Development Center
Chicago, Illinois

Sandra Hughes
Early Childhood Educator
Rainbow Express Child Care Center
Schenectady, New York

Katherine M. Lozano
Executive Director
Blessed Sacrament Academy Child Development Center
San Antonio, Texas

Marilyn Rice, M.Ed.
Director of Curriculum & Training
Tuckaway Child Development Centers
Mechanicsville, Virginia

Wendy Bertoli
Early Childhood Instructor
Lancaster County Career and Technology Center
Lancaster, Pennsylvania

Jennifer M. Johnson
Early Childhood Program Head
Vance Granville Community College
Henderson, North Carolina

Christine Pieper, MA
Director of Program Development
Petaluma, California

Bridget Murray, M.Ed.
IECE Program Coordinator
Henderson Community College
Henderson, Kentucky

Joni Levine, M.Ed.
Social Sciences Department
Community College of Allegheny County
West Mifflin, Pennsylvania

Joanne Matricardi
Jeanne McLarty

HELPFUL HINTS FOR SUCCESSFUL ACTIVITIES

Throughout the years we've developed strategies that have helped our activities to proceed more smoothly. Some are helpful behavior management tools; others deal with the preservation of materials so that they may be used year after year. The following helpful hints have become routine in our classrooms.

Prop Boxes

✄ Several activities in *Social Studies Activities A to Z* occur in the dramatic play center. Step-by-step instructions are given. However, this is only to facilitate the child's play in a new topic. The activity should be child directed.

✄ One suggestion to encourage child-directed play is the use of a prop box. Store all items related to a particular activity in a labeled box. On the day of the activity, set the items out in the dramatic play center. Play will occur naturally by adding props. It will not be necessary to dictate play.

Resource People

✄ When doing an activity, such as Nurse, it is often helpful to have a nurse visit with the class. When children enroll, you may ask parents if they will act as resource people when community helpers are presented. Seeing an actual person in their occupational role helps make the activities come alive for the children.

Behavior Management Techniques

✄ The most important aspect of working with young children is that the adults enjoy the activity. Enthusiasm is contagious. Conversely, simply going through the motions of an activity will be noticeable by the children, and their actions will reflect the adult's attitude.

✄ Be prepared. When it is time to start an activity, you should already have all the materials you need. Children will not sit still waiting for you to get ready.

✄ Maintain eye contact with the children. This helps them to sit for longer periods and keeps them interested in the activity. *However, be aware if a child's culture views eye contact as inappropriate.*

✄ When reading a book, hold the book open as you read so children can see the pictures. Know the material well enough that you can comfortably glance away from the text. It is important to spend more time looking at the children than looking at the words.

✄ Always keep the group's age and attention span in mind when planning activities. Be flexible. A group activity may need to be cut short if the attention is waning.

✄ Alternate quiet and active activities. Too many quiet plans may cause the children to lose interest. Too many active ones many cause them to become overstimulated.

Preservation of Materials

✄ When creating materials, use rubber cement for gluing; white glue may cause paper to wrinkle.

✄ If possible, laminate all materials made with paper. A laminator may be purchased for $350 to $1500. Some school supply or office supply stores will laminate materials for a set fee.

✄ If you do not have access to a laminator, use clear, unpatterned contact paper or heavy tag board.

✄ Store materials in resealable plastic bags. This allows you to see at a glance what is inside and makes storage in a filing cabinet or file box easier.

Miscellaneous

✄ Making song posters encourages all adults in the room to sing along. Adult involvement is important to encourage all the children to participate. Adults don't need to feel self-conscious regarding the quality of their singing. Children are nonjudgmental and enjoy singing as a joyful experience.

✄ Song posters are also beneficial to the preschooler. Although these children cannot read, using a poster with the song written on it provides a pre-reading enrichment as it calls attention to the printed word. The use of illustrations on the poster can also help the children to identify the song.

✄ Hang the song posters at eye level for the preschooler. Masking tape is often used to hang things on the wall. Check with the center's policies as to the type of adhesive that is approved for the walls.

✄ Some activities will work great for one group of children and not for others. This may vary from year to year. If an activity fails, do not assume it is totally the adult's responsibility. The make-up of the group may play a large role in the success of an activity. At times, an activity may work better later in the year, when the children have matured. Always take time for reflection and

Mary had a little lamb,

little lamb,

little lamb.

Mary had a little lamb,

whose fleece was

white as snow.

self-evaluation. Ask yourself, "What made the activity a success?" or "Is there something that can be improved upon?"

SAFETY PRECAUTIONS

Some of the social studies activities involve cooking. These activities may require additional safety precautions. The following practices are standard in our classrooms.

✂ Wash all fruits and vegetables thoroughly with running water. *Vegetarian Times* cautions against using soap, since the produce will absorb it (Hise, 2004).

✂ Check the center's policies. Some schools will not allow the use of heating elements in the classroom and require the adults to heat or bake food in the kitchen.

✂ When using a hot plate or electric skillet, roll towels and place around the appliance to create a buffer between the heat and the child.

✂ If adult needs to leave the room, lift the electric appliance out of reach. Make sure the cord is also out of reach.

✂ Do not leave cords plugged into an outlet once the appliance has been detached. This is like leaving an outlet uncovered.

✂ If using equipment with cords, tape the cord to the table and floor. This is to ensure the appliance doesn't get pulled off the table by a dangling cord, and also prevents people from tripping over cords on the floor.

✂ Always supervise children closely when cooking. Small foods may present a choking hazard to young children.

- ✄ Adults need to be aware of the children's allergies. There has been a growing number of children who have food allergies. Reactions to peanuts or other nuts have become more common. When nuts are used, substitutions are suggested. Milk allergies are also being seen more frequently. Rice or soy milk and vegetable "cheese" products may be exchanged for dairy products. Another common allergy is peanut butter. Some children are so highly allergic to peanut butter that they may have a reaction without touching it; merely being present in a room where it is being used is enough to cause a reaction.
- ✄ A classroom can keep an accurate and updated allergy chart that adults are able to check before beginning any activity involving food. Dietary requirements may also be kept with this chart, such as if a child is to abstain from pork or all meat products.
- ✄ A growing number of preschool children are vegetarian. Substitutions for these recipes are suggested when meat products are used. The parents of these children are usually very happy to supply the needed soy alternatives.

SUPPLIES NEEDED

Most early childhood programs operate on a limited budget. Many of the materials we use in this book may be purchased at your local dollar store. The shopping list that follows has been divided into seven categories: consumables, nonconsumables, equipment, clothing, kitchen equipment, food, and recyclable items.

CONSUMABLE SUPPLIES

Adding machine tape
Alcohol wipes
Aluminum foil
Birthday candles (red, green, black)
Bowls (assorted sizes)
Brown liquid watercolor
Candles
Cardstock paper (assorted colors)
Cellophane tape
Clear contact paper
Colored pencils
Construction paper (assorted colors and sizes)
Copy paper (assorted colors)
Cotton balls
Craft sticks
Crayons
Cups (clear, plastic)
Dirt
Dish soap
Envelopes
Film
Fine-tipped marker
Foam plates
Foam sheets (assorted colors)
Food coloring (blue and green)
Glow in the dark stars
Glue
Heavy string
Hook and loop tape
Index cards
Individually wrapped candy
Markers
Masking tape
Metal paper clips
Napkins
Notepad
Paper plates
Paper towels
Pencils
Permanent marker
Piñata
Piñata stick
Pipe cleaners
Plastic bags

Plastic knives
Plastic spoons
Poster board
Potting soil
Resealable plastic bags
   (assorted sizes)
Rubber bands
Rubber cement
Rubbing alcohol
Sand
School glue
Seeds (assorted)
Spray paint (black and gold)
Spray polyurethane
Stamps
Staples
Stickers
Sticky notes pad
Straws (assorted bright colors)
String
Tagboard
Tempera paint (assorted colors)
Tempera paint (florescent colors)
Tissue paper (assorted colors)
Tongue depressors
Toothpicks
Valentine cards with envelopes
Water
Wax paper
White chalk
White paper
White paper plates
Wool yarn
Yarn

NONCONSUMABLE SUPPLIES
12" wooden dowel
Artificial Christmas tree
Baby bottles
Balance scales
Basket
Bathroom scale
Battery-operated lantern or lamp
Bell (handheld)
Black kettle or cups
Blood pressure cuff
Box cutter
Child-size broom
Child-size dustpan
Child-size pitcher
Child-size watering can
Children's books
Chips or counters

Clear, plastic gems
Clipboard
Divided tray
Flashlight
Flower stencil
Funnel
Globe
Hairdryer with cord removed
Handkerchief
Hole punch
Holiday lights
House paint brush
Interlocking blocks
Large plastic container
Laundry baskets
Magnetic wand
Magnifying glass
Menorah
Metal rings
Mirror
Multicultural dolls
Nesting cups
Paint brushes (assorted sizes)
Paint cups
Phone cord
Plastic bat
Plastic dish pan
Plastic food
Plastic plates
Plastic smocks
Plastic yo-yos
Play money
Plunger (used only for art)
Pointer
Rocks
Ruler
Scissors (adult, heavy duty,
   and child-size)
Screwdriver (flathead)
Screwdriver (Phillips)
Shovel (adult and child-size)
Small basket
Small plastic trees
Small stuffed toy rabbit
Smocks
Sponges (assorted shapes)
Spray bottle
Spring clothespins
Stamp pad
Stamps
Stapler
State map
Stencil with flowers

Stethoscope
Stick
Stuffed animals
Towels
Toy binoculars
Toy firefighter hats
Toy stethoscope
Toy syringe
Toy telescope
Toy tractor
Tray
Tree ornaments
Tree with roots
Trowels
Tweezers
United States map
Utility knife
Washcloth
Watering hose
Wire cutters
Wooden blocks
Wooden notched logs
Yardstick

EQUIPMENT
Balance beam
Ball with minimal bounce
Bean bags
Bookshelf
Buckets (assorted sizes)
Camera
CD
CD player
Chairs
Child-size soccer goals
Cot
Crate
Globe
Paper cutter
Rhythmic ribbons
Sensory table
Small stool
Small tables
Soccer balls
Standing divider

CLOTHING
Black top hat
Brown hat
Brown shirt
Dress-up clothes
Rain coats (child-size)
Socks

White apron
White short-sleeved adult
   oxford shirt

KITCHEN EQUIPMENT
Baking sheets
Can puncher
Colander
Cookie cutters
Crock pot
Cups
Cutting board
Electric skillet
Griddle
Knives
Large plastic container with lid
Long-handled spoons
Long-handled wooden spoon
Measuring cups
Measuring spoons
Mixing bowls
Nonstick electric skillet
Pans
Pans (child-size)
Pastry cloth
Plastic plates
Pie pans
Pot holders
Pots
Quart baking dish
Rolling pin (adult-size)
Rolling pin (child-size)
Smooth edge can opener
Spatula
Tray
Vegetable peeler
Whisk

FOOD
15 oz. can black beans
46 oz. can vegetable juice
Apricots
Bananas
Bread
Butter
Buttermilk dressing
Celery
Coffee grounds
Cooking oil
Cooking spray
Corn flour
Cornmeal
Cucumber
Dried lima beans

Eggs
English muffins
Flour
Food coloring (assorted colors)
Frozen bread dough
Garlic powder
Grapes
Green onions
Lemon juice
Loose leaf tea
Mangoes
Olive oil
Pepper
Pitted black olives
Red onion
Roma tomatoes
Salt
Shredded mozzarella cheese
Sliced ham
Sliced turkey
Small cucumber

Small green bell pepper
Small red onion
Vegetable oil
Vinegar

RECYCLABLE ITEMS
Cardboard
Cardboard boxes (assorted sizes)
Child's shoe
Egg carton
Empty coffee can
Empty paper towel tubes
Empty wrapping paper tubes
Empty 16–20 oz. clear soda bottles
    with lids
Junk mail
Magazines
Newspapers
Shoe boxes with lids
Small broken appliances
Small gift boxes with lids

Airline Pilot

AGES: 3–5

GROUP SIZE:
2–4 children

DEVELOPMENTAL GOALS:
- ✂ To appreciate various occupations
- ✂ To enhance social development

LEARNING OBJECTIVE:
Using chairs, a cardboard box with holiday lights, a phone cord, and a small box, the children will take turns playing the role of an airplane pilot.

MATERIALS:
Scissors
Cardboard box
Holiday lights
Masking tape
Phone cord
Small box that will fit in a child's hand
Chairs
Paper plate

DISCUSSION SUGGESTIONS:

- ✂ A pilot may fly close to home or all over the world.
- ✂ The pilot must check many details before taking off.
- ✂ He or she has to check the instrument panel, weather, flight schedule, and other things.
- ✂ The pilot has to get permission from the control tower to take off. He or she also needs permission from the control tower to land.
- ✂ A pilot is responsible for the safety of all the passengers and crew members that are on the airplane.

ADULT PREPARATION:

1. Poke holes in the bottom of a cardboard box.
2. Insert holiday lights through the holes. Secure the lights with masking tape. This is the instrument panel.
3. Attach one end of a phone cord to the box. Attach the other end to a small box that will fit in a child's hand. This is the radio.

continued

Airline Pilot continued

4. Place chairs to resemble rows and seats in an airplane.

5. Place a separate chair in front of the others for the pilot.

6. Cut a paper plate in half. Place one half on the pilot's chair to be used as the steering wheel.

7. Plug the lights in. Tape the cord to the floor to prevent tripping.

PROCEDURES:

The children will complete the following steps:

1. Assign roles of pilot and passengers.

2. The pilot and the passengers will take their seats and buckle their imaginary seatbelts for safety.

3. The pilot will "check the instrument panel."

4. The pilot will speak through the hand-held radio asking for clearance to take off.

5. The pilot will grip the steering wheel and pretend to take-off, fly the plane, and land the plane.

6. Once the plane has landed, children may take turns with being the pilot or passenger and repeat steps 2–5.

⚠ SAFETY PRECAUTION:

Holiday lights may be hazardous for young children. Small flashlights could be used in place of holiday lights.

Arbor Day

AGES: 3–5

GROUP SIZE:
6–15 children

DEVELOPMENTAL GOALS:
- ✂ To build an appreciation of the environment
- ✂ To develop large muscles

LEARNING OBJECTIVE:
Using shovels, a tree with intact roots, watering hose, and water, the children will plant a tree.

MATERIALS:
Tree with intact roots
Shovel
Scissors
Watering hose
Water
Child-size shovels
Poster board
Yardstick
Marker

DISCUSSION SUGGESTIONS:

- ✂ *Webster's Dictionary* defines *arbor* as a shelter in a garden formed by trees (*Webster's Dictionary and Roget's Thesarus*, 2001).
- ✂ Arbor Day was founded by J. Sterling Morton in Nebraska in 1872.
- ✂ Nebraska used to be a treeless plain.
- ✂ Morton proposed the tree planting holiday to the State Board of Agriculture.
- ✂ The first Arbor Day was April 10, 1872. Counties and individuals who planted the largest number of trees, in Nebraska, were awarded prizes. More than one million trees were planted that day (The History of Arbor Day, n.d.).
- ✂ Arbor Day is celebrated on different days depending on the state. For example: In Alabama it is celebrated the last full week in February. In Alaska, Arbor Day is the third Monday in May. Refer to the Arbor Day website to find a state's date and also the state tree (*Arbor Day*, 2005).
- ✂ Arbor Day is also celebrated in Japan, Israel, Korea, Yugoslavia, Iceland, and India.

continued

Arbor Day continued

ADULT PREPARATION:

1. Purchase or ask for a donation of a tree with the roots intact.
2. Check with the supplier as to how deep the hole must be to successfully plant the tree. The depth of the hole varies with different regions.
3. Select a spot to plant the tree and dig the hole with the shovel. This needs to be within reach of the water hose.

PROCEDURES:

The children will complete the following steps:

1. Assist in placing the tree in the hole.
2. Watch the adult use scissors to cut the burlap that has bundled the roots.
3. Use a watering hose to cover the roots with water.
4. Take turns using the child-size shovels to refill the hole with dirt.
5. Take turns to pat down the dirt on the ground and around the trunk of the tree.
6. Use the hose to drench the dirt with water.

The adult will complete the following step:

1. Using poster board, yardstick, and marker, create a chart to plot the growth of the tree.

EXPANSIONS:

✄ Keep the tree watered adequately over the following months. This will involve the children in the long-term care of the tree and will strengthen their learning about the environment.

✄ Enchantedlearning.com offers craft suggestions to help celebrate Arbor Day.

4

Australia's Animal Match

DISCUSSION SUGGESTIONS:

- ✂ Different countries may have animals that are not seen in the area the child lives.
- ✂ Australia has animals that are unique to its country and some that are found in other countries.
- ✂ The Australian crocodile has a dull color that blends with its surroundings.
    - ✂ It has a long narrow snout.
    - ✂ Its nose, eyes, and ear openings are high on its head.
- ✂ The Australian spiny anteater has a long nose that looks like a bird's beak.
    - ✂ It likes to eat ants and termites.
    - ✂ It catches the insects with its long, gluey tongue.
- ✂ The bandicoot is a marsupial, which means it has a pouch for its baby like the kangaroo.
    - ✂ Bandicoots live on the ground.
    - ✂ They eat spiders, insects, and underground fungus.
    - ✂ Some are gray or brown. They have long ears.
- ✂ The dingo is like a dog or wolf.
    - ✂ It lives in the forests and grasslands.
    - ✂ The dingo never barks. It growls, howls, and whimpers.
    - ✂ The dingo first came to Australia from Asia.
- ✂ The emu is a large bird that cannot fly.
    - ✂ It is the third-largest bird in the world.
    - ✂ It can grow to six feet tall and weigh 110 pounds.
- ✂ The kangaroo is nocturnal, which means they come out mostly at night.
    - ✂ The adult male is called a buck, boomer, or jack. The adult female is called a doe, flyer, roo, or jill. The baby is called a joey.
    - ✂ The females have a pouch for the baby to live in and drink milk.

continued

A

AGES: 2–5

GROUP SIZE:
2–3 children

DEVELOPMENTAL GOALS:
- ✂ To develop an awareness of what exists beyond our boundaries
- ✂ To encourage classification skills

LEARNING OBJECTIVE:
Using Australian animal cards, the child will identify and match animals.

MATERIALS:
Australia animal patterns (Appendix A1–A8)
Australian crocodile (Appendix A1)
Australian spiny anteater (Appendix A2)
Bandicoot (Appendix A3)
Dingo (Appendix A4)
Emu (Appendix A5)
Kangaroo (Appendix A6)
Koala (Appendix A7)

Australia's Animal Match continued

MATERIALS:

Kookaburra
(Appendix A8)
Copy paper
Construction paper
Scissors
Ruler
Rubber cement
Fine-tipped permanent
marker
Globe

✄ The koala has very sharp, long claws.

  ✄ It eats two to three pounds of eucalyptus leaves daily. It also eats dirt and stones to help it digest the leaves.

  ✄ The koala never leaves the tree to drink water. It gets enough water from the leaves it eats.

  ✄ It makes a noise like a saw cutting wood.

✄ The kookaburra is a large bird.

  ✄ It makes a sound like human laughter.

  ✄ It doesn't drink water. It gets its moisture from food sources.

  ✄ It eats insects, earthworms, and small reptiles and amphibians.

(*Amazing Animals of the World*, 1995)

ADULT PREPARATION:

1. Make two copies of each Australian animal pattern.

2. Cut construction paper into sixteen 4" × 4" squares.

3. Use rubber cement to glue each Australian animal picture onto a construction paper square, creating matching cards.

4. Use a fine-tipped permanent marker to write the name of each animal on the bottom of each card.

5. When dry, lay one set of pictures face up on the table.

6. Lay the duplicate cards in a stack face down on the table.

PROCEDURES:

The child will complete the following steps:

1. Find the state he or she lives in on the globe with the adult's assistance.

2. Find Australia on the globe with the adult's assistance. Note the distance between the two.

3. Identify the animals on the table, with adult's assistance if needed.

4. Turn the top card of the stack face up.

5. Identify the card and place it with the matching animal on the table.

6. Repeat steps 4–5 until all the animals have been matched.

continued

Australia's Animal Match continued

NOTES:

- ✂ Younger two-year-olds should only start with 2–3 matches. Increase the number of cards as the child's attention span and ability increases.
- ✂ Print name of the animal on the card for older preschoolers to be able to see the word.

BOOK SUGGESTION:

Australian Wildlife from the Nature Kids series, writing and photography by Steve Parish (Philadelphia, PA: Mason Crest Publishers, 2003). The text is suitable for older preschoolers, but the pictures make it worthwhile for all ages as the unusual animals of Australia are shown in large, colorful photographs.

EXPANSION:

Make 3–6 cards of each animal and have the child sort and count them.

B

Baker

AGES: 3–5

GROUP SIZE:

2–4 children

DEVELOPMENTAL GOALS:

✂ To develop an awareness of different occupations

✂ To practice role-playing

LEARNING OBJECTIVE:

Using baking equipment and ingredients, the child will act as a baker.

MATERIALS:

Frozen bread dough
Knife
Plate
Baking sheet
Aluminum foil
Flour
Small bowl
Book about a baker
White apron
Cutting board or pastry cloth
Child-size rolling pin
Cookie cutters
Permanent marker

DISCUSSION SUGGESTIONS:

✂ A baker is a type of cook.

✂ A baker makes and sells pies, cakes, pastries, and breads.

✂ A baker must keep their hands and kitchen very clean. This helps keep the customers healthy.

✂ "What would be your favorite food to bake?"

ADULT PREPARATION:

1. Thaw bread dough in the refrigerator the night before use.

2. Wash hands.

3. Cut dough with the knife into equal pieces so there is one piece for each child. Roll into balls and place on a plate.

4. Cover a baking sheet with aluminum foil.

5. Place a small amount of flour in a small bowl.

6. Preheat the oven to 350°.

continued

8

Baker continued

PROCEDURES:

The child will complete the following steps:

1. Read book about a baker and her job.
2. Wash hands.
3. Put on apron.
4. Sprinkle flour over the cutting board or pastry cloth.
5. Rub the flour over the cutting board or cloth with hands.
6. Select a ball of dough.
7. Knead the dough into the flour.
8. Use the rolling pin to flatten the dough.
9. Select a cookie cutter and press it into the dough.
10. Lift the cookie cutter off the dough and lift up the cut dough.
11. Place the pressed dough shape onto the baking sheet.
12. With the remnants of the dough, roll it into a ball and repeat steps 6–10.

The adult will complete the following steps:

1. Make sure the dough shapes are approximately 2" apart.
2. Write the child's name under their creation(s) using the permanent marker.
3. Place in the oven and bake for 10–20 minutes. The dough is finished when it is golden brown.
4. If the children are going to eat this for snack or a meal, allow it to cool before serving.
5. Ask the children to describe the work they did as a baker.

VARIATIONS:

✂ Omit baking and let the child use play dough.
✂ Set out various baking materials and let the child pretend to measure and mix ingredients.

NOTE:

Baking times will vary due to the size of the divided dough balls.

continued

Baker continued

BOOK SUGGESTIONS:

✂ *Bread Bakery* by Catherine Anderson (Chicago, IL: Heinemann Library, 2005). This book shows the process of baking bread at the bakery with colorful photographs and simple text.

✂ Eric Carle's *Walter the Baker* (New York: Simon & Schuster Books for Young Readers, 1995). Walter makes the best sweet rolls in town until his cat spills the milk one morning and Walter is forced to substitute milk with water. The Duke and Duchess are furious and ban him from the kingdom, unless he can fulfill a specific task.

Belgium's Diamonds

B

AGES: 3–5

GROUP SIZE:
2–3 children

DEVELOPMENTAL GOALS:
- ✂ To develop a global view
- ✂ To recognize numbers

LEARNING OBJECTIVE:
Using numbered gift boxes and clear, plastic gems, the child will recognize numbers and count rationally.

MATERIALS:
12 small gift boxes with lids
Permanent marker
Clear plastic gems
Bowl
Globe

DISCUSSION SUGGESTIONS:

- ✂ Diamonds are gemstones that were formed billions of years ago.
- ✂ Antwerp is the second-largest city in Belgium. It is called the diamond center of the world. More than 70% of the world's diamonds are cut, polished, and sold there (Vantage Adventures, 2004).

ADULT PREPARATION:

1. Write numbers 0–12 on the top of the box lids.
2. Place clear plastic gems (diamonds) in a bowl.
3. Place the boxes on a table in random order.

PROCEDURES:

The child will complete the following steps:

1. Find the state he or she lives in on the globe with the adult's assistance.
2. Find Belgium on the globe with the adult's assistance. Note the distance between the two.

continued

B

Belgium's Diamonds continued

3. Identify the number on a box lid.
4. Remove the lid and count out the number of gems (diamonds) equal to the number and place them in the box.
5. Repeat steps 3–4 until all boxes except zero have received gems (diamonds).

NOTE:

For younger children, first lay out only numbers 1–3. Add to the amount of numbers as the child's skill level increases.

EXPANSIONS:

✂ In the manipulative or science area give the child large plastic tweezers and a magnifying glass to pick up diamonds and examine them.

✂ Set up a diamond store in the dramatic play area to sell and buy diamonds. Display the gems on a black cloth or black construction paper. Use small boxes, a cash register, and play money as additional props.

⚠ SAFETY PRECAUTION:

Supervise children carefully when using small items to prevent choking.

Bus Driver

AGES: 3–5

GROUP SIZE:
2–6 children

DEVELOPMENTAL GOALS:
- ✂ To identify occupations in our community
- ✂ To promote role playing

LEARNING OBJECTIVE:
Using chairs, a small stool, a money box, and a plate, the children will role-play bus driver and passengers.

MATERIALS:
Shoe box with lid
Box cutter
Chairs
Small stool
Plastic plate
Book about a bus driver
Play money

DISCUSSION SUGGESTIONS:
- ✂ Bus drivers give people rides to help them get to where they need to go.
- ✂ The drivers have to follow a specific route. They have to drive their routes at specific times.
- ✂ Bus drivers have to drive safely and follow traffic rules.
- ✂ Drivers talk to people as they get on and off the bus. When the bus is moving, the driver needs to concentrate on driving.

ADULT PREPARATION:
1. Cut a slot in the top of the shoe box lid large enough for money to slip through.
2. Line chairs up in two rows resembling a bus.

continued

Bus Driver continued

3. Place a single chair in front of all the other chairs for the driver.

4. Set the small stool beside the driver's seat. Place the shoe box, with lid, on the stool.

5. Set a plastic plate on the driver's seat for a steering wheel.

PROCEDURES:

The children will complete the following steps:

1. Listen to the adult read a story about riding on a bus.

2. Discuss bus safety:

   a. Sit on bus.

   b. Wait until the bus stops before standing up.

3. Children will take turns playing the roles of bus driver or passengers.

4. Passengers will be given money to pay their fare.

5. The driver will take his seat on the bus.

6. The driver will pick up the steering wheel and pretend to drive.

7. The driver will stop and pick up passengers.

8. The passengers will enter the bus and drop their fare into the shoe box.

9. After paying for their seat, the passengers will sit down.

10. The driver will continue driving.

11. The driver will drop off passengers and pick up others.

12. The children will change roles, and steps 4–10 will be repeated.

BOOK SUGGESTION:

Maisy Drives the Bus by Lucie Cousins (Cambridge, MA: Candlewick Press, 2000). Maisy drives the bus and makes various stops. At each stop, one of her friends boards the bus.

EXPANSION:

Sing *Wheels on the Bus*.

Chef

DISCUSSION SUGGESTIONS:

✂ A baker makes pies, cakes, and pastries. A chef is the chief cook in a kitchen.

✂ A chef may have a large kitchen staff.

✂ Safety tips chefs must follow:

  ✂ Wash hands before and after handling food.

  ✂ Wash fruits and vegetables before cooking.

  ✂ Only use sharp utensils, electrical appliances, and hot pots and pans with adult help.

  ✂ Use pot holders when handling hot pots and pans.

  ✂ Clean up work area and all cooking utensils.

ADULT PREPARATION:

1. For each child, roll white construction paper into a tube large enough to fit the child's head.

2. Staple the construction paper tube to create a chef's hat.

3. Write each child's name on individual hats using a marker.

4. Set out pot holders, plastic plates, pans, plastic food, and utensils.

PROCEDURES:

The children will complete the following steps:

1. Listen to the adult read a book about a chef and the job.

2. Put the chef's hat and apron on.

3. Select food to cook.

4. If plastic fruits and vegetables are used, pretend to wash them.

5. Put the food in a pan, stir it with the long-handled spoon or whisk.

6. Select different food. Use a spatula to flip the food in the pan.

7. Use the hot pad when handling hot pots and pans.

8. When food is cooked, use a spatula to put it on a plastic plate.

9. Pretend to clean work area and wash pots and pans.

BOOK SUGGESTION:

Chop, Simmer, Season by Alexa Brandenberg (New York: Harcourt Brace and Co., 1997). This book uses words and short phrases to talk about how chefs prepare food.

AGES: 3–5

GROUP SIZE:
2–3 children

DEVELOPMENTAL GOALS:

✂ To appreciate different occupations

✂ To encourage imagination through role-playing

LEARNING OBJECTIVE:
Using a chef's hat, plastic plates, pans, plastic food, and utensils, the children will pretend to be a chef.

MATERIALS:
White construction paper (18" × 24")
Stapler and staples
Marker
Pot holders
Plastic plates
Pans
Plastic food
Long-handled spoon
Whisk
Spatula
Book about a chef
White apron

Chinese Panda Bear

AGES: 3–5

GROUP SIZE:
2–3 children

DEVELOPMENTAL GOALS:
- ✄ To develop awareness of animals in other countries
- ✄ To enhance fine motor control

LEARNING OBJECTIVE:
Using a picture of a panda bear, blue construction paper, various sizes of circle sponges, paint blotter, and smock, the child will attempt to create a panda bear.

MATERIALS:
Copy paper
Chinese panda bear pattern (Appendix A10)
Pencil
White construction paper
White and black tempera paint
Foam plates
Spoon

DISCUSSION SUGGESTIONS:
- ✄ The panda bear is an endangered animal found in China.
- ✄ *Endangered* means there aren't many left and they are in danger of becoming extinct. If panda bears become extinct, there will not be any living panda bears on Earth.
- ✄ The panda bear is known for its black-and-white coloring.
- ✄ It eats a lot of bamboo every day.

ADULT PREPARATION:
1. Make a copy of the pattern of the Chinese panda bear.
2. Cut one panda bear for each child on white construction paper.
3. Pour white tempera paint and black tempera paint onto separate foam plates.
4. Add 1 spoonful of dish soap and mix into paint.
5. Put a paper towel on top of the paint.

continued

Chinese Panda Bear continued

6. Flip the towel over creating a paint blotter, which limits the amount of paint the sponge may absorb.
7. Dampen the circle sponges with water and place them on the paint blotter.
8. Cover the table with newspaper.

PROCEDURES:

The child will complete the following steps:

1. Find the state he or she lives in on the globe with the adult's assistance.
2. Find China on the globe with the adult's assistance. Note the distance between the two.
3. Listen to a book about a panda bear.
4. Answer the question, "What color is a panda bear?"
5. Wearing a smock, dip the sponges into the paint.
6. Press the sponges onto the panda bear cutout.
7. Repeat steps 5–6.

BOOK SUGGESTION:

Pi-shu, the Little Panda by John Butler (Atlanta, GA: Peachtree Publishers, 2001). Pi-shu is a baby panda who wanders to the edge of the forest only to find men chopping down all the trees. The forest isn't safe anymore, and Pi-shu and his mother must find another place to live.

MATERIALS:

Dish soap
Paper towels
Various sizes of circle sponges
Newspaper
Globe
Book about a panda bear
Smocks

Danish Smørrebrød

GROUP SIZE:

4–16 children

DEVELOPMENTAL GOALS:

✂ To appreciate the culture from another country

✂ To make a nutritious snack

LEARNING OBJECTIVE:

Using ingredients and kitchen supplies, the children will make a Danish food.

MATERIALS:

Bread (sliced thin)
Plates
Butter or margarine
Plastic knives
Sliced ham or turkey

DISCUSSION SUGGESTIONS:

✂ Denmark is a country in northern Europe.

✂ Hans Christian Andersen is from Denmark. He wrote *The Ugly Duckling* and many other stories.

✂ Danish people eat four meals a day: breakfast, lunch, dinner, and supper.

✂ Dinner is usually the only meal that is hot.

✂ A favorite Danish dish is *smørrebrød* (**smurrer**-brurth).

✂ *Smørrebrød* is a thin piece of bread spread with butter and topped with meat (Britton, 2004).

ADULT PREPARATION:

1. Wash hands.

2. Put a thin slice of bread on individual plates—one for each child.

3. Put approximately 1 teaspoon of butter or margarine to the side of each plate.

4. Place a slice of meat on each plate.

continued

Danish Smørrebrød continued

PROCEDURES:

The children will complete the following steps:

1. Find the state the children live in on the globe with the adult's assistance.
2. Find Denmark on the globe with the adult's assistance. Note the distance between the two.
3. Wash hands.
4. Spread butter on the bread with a plastic knife.
5. Put a slice of meat on top.
6. Cut the *smørrebrød* in half if desired.
7. Eat the *smørrebrød* for snack or lunch.

VEGETARIAN VARIATION:

Ask parents to provide a soy product resembling a sliced meat, such as meatless "turkey."

SAFETY PRECAUTIONS:

Check for allergies before beginning any activity with food.

December Holidays

* Holidays are an important part of Social Studies for young children.
* Acknowledging how other cultures celebrate holidays is a start to understanding and appreciating diversity.
* Children must understand that even when people celebrate differently, it is not wrong; it is simply different.

I. DECEMBER HOLIDAY: CHRISTMAS ITEMS MATCH

DISCUSSION SUGGESTIONS:

* Some people celebrate Christmas on December 25th.
* People who celebrate Christmas may put up a Christmas tree and decorate it with ornaments. There are many different kinds of ornaments to put on a tree.

ADULT PREPARATION:

1. Take and develop pictures of tree ornaments.
2. Place pictures in a basket.
3. Set up small artificial tree.
4. Place ornaments on a tray.

continued

AGES: 3–5

GROUP SIZE:
2–10 children

DEVELOPMENTAL GOALS:

* To value and appreciate people across cultures
* To develop classification skills

LEARNING OBJECTIVE:

Using tree ornaments, pictures, a basket, tray, and a small artificial tree, the children will take turns matching and decorating a tree with ornaments.

MATERIALS:

Tree ornaments
Camera and film, or digital camera
Basket
Small artificial tree
Tray

22

December Holidays continued

PROCEDURES:

The children will complete the following steps:

1. Sit in a circle or semicircle.
2. Take turns completing the following:
   a. Select one picture out of the basket.
   b. Find the matching Christmas ornament on the tray.
   c. Place the ornament on the tree.
3. Repeat step 2 until all children have participated.

 ## SAFETY PRECAUTION:

Use unbreakable ornaments without wire hooks.

NOTE:

If not all children celebrate Christmas, have other holiday decorations such as the Star of David for Jewish children or generic holiday décor such as hearts, bears, bells, etc.

BOOK SUGGESTION:

Christmas is . . . by Gail Gibbons (New York: Holiday House, 2001). The different aspects of Christmas are explained in this book.

2. DECEMBER HOLIDAY: HANUKKAH MENORAH

continued

AGES: 3–5

GROUP SIZE:
3–5 children

DEVELOPMENTAL GOALS:

✂ To develop an appreciation for their own ways and the ways of others

✂ To enhance eye-hand coordination

December Holidays continued

DISCUSSION SUGGESTIONS:

- ✂ Hanukkah is one of the celebrations of the Jewish religion.
- ✂ It is celebrated for eight nights. All Jewish holidays start at sunset.
- ✂ Hanukkah is called the Festival of Lights.
- ✂ The tall middle candle on the Menorah is called the *Shamash*. *Shamash* means leader. Its location on the Menorah is taller than or separate from the other eight candles or it may be visually different. A new *Shamash* is lit first every night.
- ✂ The *Shamash* is lit the night before the first of the eight nights of Hanukkah.
- ✂ The first night one candle is put in the menorah on the right. The *Shamash* is lit and then it lights the first candle.
- ✂ The second night, a new *Shamash* is put in. Two candles are put in on the right. The *Shamash* is lit and it is used to light the other candles from left to right (newest candle first).
- ✂ This continues for a total of eight nights, with an additional candle put in each night. Candles are always put in from the right, but lit from the left.

ADULT PREPARATION:

1. Cut a rectangle 1" × 7" for each child using brown construction paper.
2. Cut a rectangle 2" × 9" for each child using brown construction paper.
3. Copy and cut nine flames for each child using orange construction paper.
4. Pour brown tempera paint into a paint cup, mixing it with 1–2 tablespoons of dish soap.

PROCEDURES:

The child will complete the following steps:

1. Listen to a story read about Hanukkah.
2. Set the candles in the menorah.
3. Put on a smock.
4. Glue the 2" × 9" rectangle at the bottom of the construction paper.

continued

December Holidays continued

5. Glue the 1″ × 7″ rectangle in the center of the other rectangle at a perpendicular angle.

6. Using a paintbrush, paint four fingers of the nondominant hand brown, with adult assistance if needed.

7. Press the fingers to the left of the upright rectangle while touching the horizontal rectangle, with adult assistance if needed.

8. Repeat steps 4 and 5, pressing the painted fingers to the right of the upright rectangle while touching the horizontal rectangle.

9. Wash and dry hands.

10. Glue a flame on top of each finger and on top of the vertical rectangle.

Note: This activity and discussion suggestions were provided by Jill Burnham of Snellville, Georgia.

VARIATION:

Use tissue paper tubes for the eight candles and a paper towel tube for the center candle. Paint and glue the tubes on a strip of cardboard. Stuff the tubes with orange or yellow tissue paper for flames.

NOTES:

✄ If a sink is not in the classroom, a bucket of soapy water and paper towels may be used for clean up.

✄ Older children may trace and cut the rectangles and flames.

BOOK SUGGESTION:

Hanukkah Lights by Lee Bennett Hopkins (New York: HarperCollins Publishers, Inc., 2004). This book of poetry celebrates Hanukkah, featuring poems such as "Latke Time," "Five Little Dreidels," and "One Little Miracle."

continued

December Holidays continued

AGES: 3–5

GROUP SIZE:

2–3 children

DEVELOPMENTAL GOALS:

✄ To value and appreciate people across cultures

✄ To stimulate small muscle development

LEARNING OBJECTIVE:

Using dough and candles, the child will create a kinara.

MATERIALS:

Measuring cup
Flour
Salt
Mixing bowls
Brown liquid watercolor
Hot water
Spoon
Teaspoon
Vegetable oil
Bowl
Baking sheet

3. DECEMBER HOLIDAY: KWANZAA

DISCUSSION SUGGESTIONS:

✄ The candles are called *mishumma*.

✄ On the first day of Kwanzaa, the black candle is lit.

✄ An additional candle is lit for each successive day.

✄ On the second day, the red candle next to the black one is lit. On the third day, the green candle next to the black one is also lit, and so on.

ADULT PREPARATION:

1. Measure 4 cups of flour and 1 cup of salt into a mixing bowl.

2. Mix brown liquid water color into 1¼ cups of hot water.

3. Stir in 2 teaspoons of vegetable oil.

4. Add the liquid to the flour and salt. Mix well.

5. The consistency of the dough should be elastic. If it is too dry, add a little more water. If it is too sticky, add more flour.

6. Divide the dough into equal pieces and place them in a bowl.

7. Cover a baking sheet with aluminum foil.

8. Preheat the oven to 200°.

continued

December Holidays continued

PROCEDURES:

The child will complete the following steps:

1. Listen to book read about Kwanzaa.
2. Wash hands.
3. Select a piece of dough.
4. Roll the dough into a "snake." Make sure it is flat on the bottom.
5. Use a birthday candle to push seven holes into the dough. This will be the *kinara* (candle holder). Do not leave the candles in the dough.
6. Place the *kinara* on the foil covered baking sheet.

The adult will complete the following steps:

1. Write the child's name on the foil, under their *kinara*, with a permanent marker.
2. Once the baking sheet is full, bake the dough until it is hard. Baking times will vary depending upon the thickness of the dough.
3. When the dough is hard, remove it from the oven and allow cooling.
4. Seal the *kinara* with spray polyurethane.

The child will complete the following steps:

1. Put a black candle in the center hole of the *kinara*.
2. Put three red candles to the right of the black candle.
3. Put three green candles to the left of the black candle.

BOOK SUGGESTION:

My First Kwanzaa Book by Deborah M. Newton Chocolate (New York: Scholastic, Inc., 1992). In this simple text and colorful pictures, a boy celebrates Kwanzaa with his family. A glossary of symbols and words used during Kwanzaa is found at the end of the book.

MATERIALS:

Aluminum foil
Book about Kwanzaa
Red, green, and black birthday candles
Permanent marker
Spray polyurethane

Dentist

GROUP SIZE:

2–3 children

DEVELOPMENTAL GOALS:

- ✄ To stimulate emotional development by lessening fear of the dentist
- ✄ To role-play life's situations

LEARNING OBJECTIVE:

Using a white short-sleeved adult oxford shirt, a dental book, chair, and dental bib, the children will role-play dentist and patient.

MATERIALS:

Scissors
Yarn
Ruler
Two spring clothespins
Napkin (one for each child)
Book about going to the dentist
White short-sleeved adult oxford shirt
Chair
Mirror

DISCUSSION SUGGESTIONS:

- ✄ Most children start going to the dentist at age three.
- ✄ For good dental health, a person should go to the dentist every six months.
- ✄ Dentists clean teeth and make sure a person doesn't have any cavities or other problems.

ADULT PREPARATION:

1. Cut yarn into 12" lengths.
2. Tie each end of yarn to a spring clothespin. This will attach to a napkin.

PROCEDURES:

The children will complete the following steps:

1. Sit in a circle or semicircle.
2. Listen to the adult read a story about going to the dentist.
3. Assign roles of dentist and patient.
4. Dentist puts on white shirt like a lab coat.
5. Patient sits in chair.
6. Dentist puts napkin on patient by placing the yarn behind their neck and then clipping the napkin on both sides to the spring clothespins.
7. Dentist has patient open mouth wide and counts teeth.
8. Dentist holds mirror for patient to see his or her teeth.

BOOK SUGGESTIONS:

- ✄ *My First Visit to the Dentist* by Monica Hughes (Chicago: Raintree, 2004). Full-size color photographs follow a little girl through her first visit to the dentist.
- ✄ *Going to the Dentist* by Helen Frost (Mankato, MN: Capstone Press, 1999). This introductory book shows the equipment the dentist uses, including the chair, tools, and lamp. It also uses full-page color photographs.

28

Easter Egg Roll at the White House

AGES: 3–5

GROUP SIZE:
2–4 children

DEVELOPMENTAL GOALS:

✂ To develop pride in cultural heritage

✂ To promote muscle development

LEARNING OBJECTIVE:
Using a boiled egg, tinted water, and a spoon, the child will color an egg and then use it in an egg roll.

MATERIALS:
Spray paint
Eggs (at least one per child)
Pan
Water
Cups
Egg carton
Permanent marker
Tablespoon
Vinegar
Food coloring
Spoons
Newspaper
Smock
Long-handled spoons

DISCUSSION SUGGESTIONS:

✂ The first White House Easter Egg Roll was held in 1878 when Rutherford B. Hayes was President (*History of the Easter Egg Roll*).

✂ The current egg rolls at the White House are more than just rolling eggs. There is also egg coloring, art activities, face painting, and music.

✂ Storytelling and reading corners are also featured at the White House Easter Egg Roll. Authors of children's books may read their work, or the reading may be done by the First Lady, White House officials, or Cabinet members.

✂ People must have a ticket to attend the Easter Egg Roll at the White House. As many as 16,000 people attend this event (2006 White House Easter Egg Roll, 2006).

ADULT PREPARATION:

1. Spray paint a start and a finish line on the playground's grass.
2. Boil at least one egg per child.

continued

Easter Egg Roll at the White House continued

3. Return boiled eggs to the carton.

4. When cool enough to handle, write each child's name on an individual egg with a permanent marker.

5. Fill cups ⅔ full with hot water and 1 tablespoon vinegar.

6. Add a different color of food coloring to each cup and stir well.

7. Cover the table with newspaper.

PROCEDURES:

The child will complete the following steps:

1. Put on a smock.

2. Select an egg from the carton with their name.

3. Using a spoon, lower the egg into the colored water of their choice.

4. Count to 30, with adult's help if needed.

5. Raise the egg with a spoon to check the color.

6. If the color is the desired hue, remove the egg from the mixture and place it back in the carton, with the adult's assistance if needed.

7. If the egg is not the desired color, place the egg back in one of the cups of colored water.

The adult will complete the following step:

1. When the eggs are dry, carry the carton to the grassy area of the playground.

The child will complete the following steps:

1. Select their egg from the carton.

2. Line up on the starting line.

3. Bend over and roll the egg along the ground with a long-handled spoon.

4. Continue rolling the egg until the finish line is reached.

SAFETY PRECAUTION:

Always wash hands before and after handling eggs.

NOTES:

✂ Sometimes eggs crack when boiling. Therefore it is a good idea to boil more than one egg per child.

✂ Plastic eggs may be used for the egg roll in place of boiled eggs.

Egypt's Pyramids

DISCUSSION SUGGESTIONS:

- ✀ Pyramids are built out of stones.
- ✀ Ancient Egyptian kings were called *pharaohs*; they built and were buried in pyramids.
- ✀ The shape of pyramids resembles the rays of the sun shining through the clouds.
- ✀ The tips of some of the pyramids were covered in gold to make them shine like the sun (Putnam, 1994).

ADULT PREPARATION:

1. Duplicate the pyramid pattern.
2. Set the pyramid picture and globe in the block area.

PROCEDURES:

The children will complete the following steps:

1. Look at the pictures in a book about pyramids.
2. Find the state the children live in on the globe with the adult's assistance.
3. Find Egypt on the globe with the adult's assistance. Note the distance between the two.
4. Take turns visiting the block area.
5. Once in the block area, look at the picture of the pyramid.
6. Attempt to build a pyramid.

BOOK SUGGESTION:

Eyewitness Pyramid by James Putnam (New York: Dorling Kindersley Publishing, Inc., 2004). This book features photographs of Egyptian pyramids and artifacts. The text is appropriate for school-age children, but it is worthwhile to share the photographs with preschoolers.

AGES: 3–5

GROUP SIZE:
2–4 children

DEVELOPMENTAL GOALS:

- ✀ To develop an awareness of geography
- ✀ To coordinate large and small muscles

LEARNING OBJECTIVE:
Using a globe, picture of a pyramid, and wooden blocks, the child will build a pyramid.

MATERIALS:
Pyramid pattern (Appendix A12)
Copy paper
Globe
Wooden blocks
Book about the pyramids

31

E

AGES: 2¹/₂–5

GROUP SIZE:

6–16 children

DEVELOPMENTAL GOALS:

✂ To promote emotional development

✂ To develop a sense of self

LEARNING OBJECTIVE:

Using emotion sticks, the child will identify different emotions.

MATERIALS:

Circle stencil (3" in diameter)
Pen or pencil
Construction paper
Scissors
Markers
Laminator or clear contact paper
Craft sticks
Stapler and staples
Small basket
Poster board
Masking tape
Book about emotions

Emotions

DISCUSSION SUGGESTIONS:

✂ People experience many different emotions.

✂ Emotions are how we react to things.

✂ Some days we might feel happy, sad, afraid, or silly.

✂ Some days we might feel up one moment and down another.

ADULT PREPARATION:

1. Trace at least six circle shapes onto construction paper. One circle should be traced for each child in the class.

2. Cut out the circles and draw different features on each circle to represent the following emotions:

   a. Happy

   b. Sad

   c. Angry

   d. Surprised

   e. Scared

   f. Silly

3. Laminate the circles, or cover them with clear contact paper.

4. Staple each circle to a craft stick.

continued

Emotions continued

5. Put each *emotion stick* into a small basket.

6. Write the words to *Emotions* on a poster board. Place it on the wall with masking tape.

PROCEDURES:

The children will complete the following steps:

1. Listen to a book read about emotions.

2. Take turns pulling an *emotion stick* out of the basket.

3. Identify the emotion on the circle and attempt to make that facial expression.

4. Once every child has selected one from the basket, hold up the emotion stick when that specific emotion is mentioned as the following chant is said:

Emotions

Happy face, happy face, what do you see?

I see an angry face looking at me.

Angry face, angry face, what do you see?

I see a surprised face looking at me.

Surprised face, surprised face, what do you see?

I see a sad face looking at me.

Sad face, sad face, looking at me, what do you see?

I see a scared face looking at me.

Scared face, scared face, what do you see?

I see a silly face looking at me.

Silly face, silly face, what do you see?

I see a happy face looking at me.

NOTES:

✄ More emotions may be used than those listed.

✄ Older children may draw the faces on the circles.

✄ Photographs of the children making emotional faces may be used in place of the drawn circles.

continued

Emotions continued

BOOK SUGGESTIONS:

✂ *On Monday When it Rained* by Cherryl Kachenmeista (New York: Houghton Mifflin Co., 1989). A little boy expresses his feelings through photos about events that happen during the week.

✂ *Walter Was Worried* by Laura Vaccaro Seeger (New Milford, CT: Roaring Brook Press, 2005). This book shows different individual's emotions through facial illustrations and statements of what elicits that feeling.

EXPANSION:

Adult may ask children what makes them happy, scared, angry, and so on.

Families

AGES: 3–5

GROUP SIZE:
2–5 children

DEVELOPMENTAL GOALS:
- ✂ To develop an awareness of belonging to a family
- ✂ To participate in a group project

LEARNING OBJECTIVE:
Using a family picture, construction paper, markers, and glue, the child will help create a class family book.

MATERIALS:
Family Letter 1 (Appendix B1)
Copy paper
Family picture
White paper
Ruler
Scissors
Fine-tipped marker
Markers
Construction paper
Glue
Laminator or clear contact paper
Hole punch
Two metal rings

DISCUSSION SUGGESTIONS:
- ✂ There are all kinds of families.
- ✂ Some families have one parent, some have two.
- ✂ Some children live with a parent and stepparent.
- ✂ Some children live with one or two grandparents.
- ✂ Other children live with parents and grandparents.
- ✂ Some children have brothers and sisters, other don't.
- ✂ Some children may live with cousins. These cousins might feel like brothers and sisters.
- ✂ Other children live with friends who become their family.

ADULT PREPARATION:
1. Send home a family letter requesting a picture of each child's family and their names and relationships.
2. Cut white paper into 2″ × 6″ rectangles.
3. Using a fine tipped marker write the child's first name with an apostrophe *s* then *Family* on the rectangle (e.g., Jacob's Family).

PROCEDURES:
The child will complete the following steps:
1. Decorate the construction paper with markers.
2. Glue his or her family picture on the paper.

continued

Families continued

3. Glue the family name under the picture (e.g., Jacob's Family).

4. Answer the adult's question, "What do you like to do with your family?"

5. Watch as the adult writes the response on a blank piece of copy paper.

The adult will complete the following steps:

1. Create a cover page out of construction paper with the title *Our Families*.

2. Laminate the cover page or cover it with clear contact paper.

3. Once the picture pages are dry, glue the dictation on the back of the child's picture page. Laminate them, or cover them with clear contact paper.

4. Punch a hole 3" from each end of the top of the picture page and cover.

5. Fasten all pages into a book by slipping two metal rings through the holes.

NOTE:

A picture may be taken of the child at drop-off or pick-up time with their parents. This may not involve the entire family, but it would ensure that a picture would be provided for each child and therefore no one would be excluded. Make sure to have a copy of a permission form to be photographed on file for each child (see Appendix B2).

BOOK SUGGESTION:

Families by Ann Morris (New York: HarperCollins Publishers, 2000). Photographs of diverse families throughout the world are shown.

EXPANSIONS:

✄ Read the book together at group time and then leave it on the shelf for children to look at independently.

✄ Children may take turns taking the book home to read with their families.

Farmers

DISCUSSION SUGGESTIONS:

✂ Farmers work outdoors.

✂ Some farmers have crops of vegetables or fruits.

✂ Some farmers have animals. A dairy farmer has cows.

✂ Some farmers plant crops and have animals.

✂ "If you were a farmer, what would you do?"

ADULT PREPARATION:

1. Place dirt in a sensory table or large plastic container.
2. Place dried lima beans in a bowl.

PROCEDURES:

The children will complete the following steps:

1. Listen to a story about planting on the farm.
2. Take turns at the sensory table where they will:
   a. Wash hands and put on a smock.
   b. Move dirt with the trowels, spoon, or tractor.
   c. Smooth the dirt into rows.
   d. Plant the lima beans in the rows.
   e. Cover the rows with dirt.
   f. Optional: Remove lima beans with a sieve so the next child(ren) will be able to plant their own beans.

⬢ SAFETY PRECAUTION:

Supervise children carefully when using small items, such as lima beans, to prevent choking.

NOTE:

Hands should be washed before and after participating in sensory table use. Washing hands before play ensures fewer germs will be put into the table's materials.

continued

F

AGES: 3–5

GROUP SIZE:
2–3 children

DEVELOPMENTAL GOALS:

✂ To appreciate nature

✂ To develop respect for different occupations

LEARNING OBJECTIVE:

Using a sensory table or large plastic container with dirt, a toy tractor, trowels or spoons, dried lima beans, and smocks, the children will act out the role of a farmer planting seeds.

MATERIALS:

Dirt
Sensory table or large plastic container
Dried lima beans
Bowl
Book about farmers
Smocks
Trowels
Spoons
Toy tractor
Optional: Sieve

Farmers continued

BOOK SUGGESTION:

We Need Farmers by Gail Saunders-Smith (Mankato, MN: Pebble Books, 2000). Color photographs and short-sentence text describe what farmers do in the community.

Firefighter

AGES: 3–5

GROUP SIZE:
2–3 children

DEVELOPMENTAL GOALS:
✂ To explore community helpers
✂ To develop interpersonal skills

LEARNING OBJECTIVE:
Using pretend water hoses, toy fire fighter's helmets, and raincoats, the children will take turns being firefighters.

MATERIALS:
Blue tissue paper
Empty wrapping paper tubes
Red, yellow, and orange tissue paper
Stapler and staples
Ruler
Scissors
Book about fire fighters
Toy fire fighter's hats
Raincoats

DISCUSSION SUGGESTIONS:
✂ Firefighters have special training and practice how to fight fires.
✂ They may sleep at the fire station.

continued

Firefighter continued

- ✂ They have to check the truck and all the tools.
- ✂ The alarm rings to let them know they need to get their gear and go fight a fire.
- ✂ Firefighters may spray water on fires.
- ✂ Some ride on fire trucks; others fight forest fires with a helicopter.
- ✂ Fire fighters may also help people when a car has been in an accident, or when a person is sick or hurt.
- ✂ Fire fighters teach about fire safety (Catala, 2004).

ADULT PREPARATION:

1. Place 2 or 3 sheets of blue tissue paper in one end of each wrapping paper tube. This is now a fire hose squirting water.
2. Layer red, yellow, and orange tissue paper together. Cut into 12" squares.
3. Create a flame by pinching the layered tissue square in the middle and smoothing the tissue together in an upward motion. Staple the center together.
4. Place the "flames" throughout the dramatic play area.

PROCEDURES:

The children will complete the following steps:

1. Listen to a story about a firefighter.
2. Take turns playing firefighters in dramatic play where they will:
   a. Put on the fire hat and raincoat.
   b. Use the water hose to put out the flames.

NOTE:

Toy firefighter hats may be purchased at party supply stores or ordered through discount companies such as *Oriental Trading*.

BOOK SUGGESTIONS:

- ✂ *Fire Fighter Piggy Wiggy* by Christyan and Diane Fox (Brooklyn, NY: Handprint Books, 2001). This book contains large colorful pictures as Piggy Wiggy imagines being a fire fighter.

continued

Firefighter continued

✂ *Fire Fighters A to Z* by Chris Demorest (New York: Simon & Schuster Children's Publishing, 2003). The steps of real fire fighters are chronicled as they fight a fire using the alphabet.

EXPANSION:

Use a telephone to practice calling 911. Children must realize this number is only called in the event of an emergency.

G

AGES: 3–5

GROUP SIZE:

2–4 children

DEVELOPMENTAL GOALS:

- ✄ To develop an appreciation of the environment
- ✄ To develop fine motor skills

LEARNING OBJECTIVE:

Using seeds, potting soil, a trowel or spoon, cup, child-size watering can with water, and a smock, the child will plant seeds like a gardener.

MATERIALS:

Cups
Permanent marker
Potting soil
Bowls
Seeds
Child-size watering can
Water
Newspaper
Smock
Trowel or spoon

Gardener

DISCUSSION SUGGESTIONS:

- ✄ A garden is a piece of land used to grow plants. The plants might be flowers, vegetables, fruits, or herbs.
- ✄ A gardener is someone who is employed to work in a garden.
- ✄ Some gardeners do not work for pay. It is a hobby for some people. They enjoy having a garden at or near their home.
- ✄ This is different from a farmer. A farmer is a person who works on or operates a farm. A farm is a large piece of land used to grow crops and/or raise animals.

ADULT PREPARATION:

1. Write child's name on a cup using a permanent marker.
2. Place potting soil and a spoon in a bowl.
3. Pour seeds into a bowl.
4. Put water in the child-size watering can.
5. Cover the table with newspaper.

PROCEDURES:

The child will complete the following steps:

1. Put on smock.
2. Find cup with his or her name.
3. Spoon potting soil into the cup, filling the cup ⅔ full.
4. Place several seeds on top of the soil.
5. Spoon more potting soil on top of the seeds, leaving at least 1" of space at the top of the cup.
6. Use the watering can to put water in the cup.
7. Place the cup in an area where it will get sunlight.
8. Check on the progress of the plant each day; water it if needed.

⊘ SAFETY PRECAUTION:

Supervise children carefully when using small items, such as seeds, to prevent choking.

continued

42

Gardener continued

NOTES:

- ✂ Dried lima beans grow very quickly.
- ✂ Plant seeds in additional cups in case a child's plant fails to grow. After the plant starts to grow, send it home with the child so he or she may continue to watch it grow at home.

BOOK SUGGESTION:

A Gardener's Alphabet by Mary Azarian (Boston, MA: Houghton Mifflin Company, 2000). Caldecott Medalist Mary Azarian's woodblock prints are featured with an alphabet of vocabulary words specific to gardening.

G

Grandparents

AGES: 3–5

GROUP SIZE:
2–10 children

DEVELOPMENTAL GOALS:
- ✄ To respect older people
- ✄ To consider the feelings of others

LEARNING OBJECTIVE:
Using a book about grandparents, paper, markers, colored pencils, or crayons, the child will mail a letter and picture to grandparents.

MATERIALS:
Family Letter 2 (Appendix B3)
Book about grandparents
Pen or pencil
Paper
Markers, colored pencils, or crayons
Stamped, addressed envelope

DISCUSSION SUGGESTIONS:

- ✄ A grandparent is the mother or father of your mother or father. It is
  - ✄ Your mom's mom or your mom's dad
  - ✄ Your dad's dad or your dad's mom
- ✄ If a child doesn't have a grandparent close by, a special older friend can be a grandparent.
- ✄ President Jimmy Carter proclaimed the first Sunday after Labor Day as Grandparents' Day in 1978.

ADULT PREPARATION:

1. Send home a family letter asking for a stamped envelope addressed to the child's grandparents.
2. If a child doesn't have grandparents, contact a local nursing home and ask for the names of residents who would like mail.

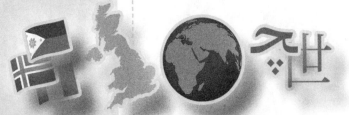

continued

Grandparents continued

PROCEDURES:

The child will complete the following steps:

1. Listen to the adult read a book about grandparents.
2. Participate in a discussion about where his or her grandparents live.
3. If he or she doesn't have any grandparents, discuss how different grandparents live in nursing homes and like to receive letters.
4. Dictate a letter, with adult prompting if necessary, as the adult will write down the words on paper.
5. Draw a picture to accompany the letter.
6. Put the picture and letter in the stamped envelope.

The adult will complete the following steps:

1. Address the envelopes going to the nursing home. Add a stamp to each envelope.
2. Mail the envelopes for all the grandparents.

BOOK SUGGESTIONS:

✂ *Song and Dance Man* by Karen Ackerman (New York: Alfred A. Knopf, 1988). Grandfather entertains his grandchildren with his old vaudeville act in this Caldecott winner illustrated by Stephen Gammell.

✂ *Grandfather's Journey* is also a Caldecott winner written by Allen Say (Boston, MA: Houghton Mifflin Company, 1993). Grandfather travels back and forth between his two loves: Japan and the United States.

Greek Pizza

AGES: 3–5

GROUP SIZE:
3–5 children

DEVELOPMENTAL GOALS:
- ✂ To appreciate another culture
- ✂ To make a nutritious snack

LEARNING OBJECTIVE:
Using ingredients, spoons, and a plate, the child will make an individual Greek pizza.

MATERIALS:
Buttermilk dressing
Measuring cup
1 stick softened butter
Garlic powder
Measuring spoons
Knife
Cutting board
Pitted black olives
Bowls
Green onions
Ham slices
Shredded mozzarella cheese
English muffins
Foam plates
Baking sheet

DISCUSSION SUGGESTIONS:

- ✂ Greek pizza refers to two styles of pizza.
- ✂ One pizza uses Greek ingredients such as feta cheese, gyro meat, Kalamata olives, and spinach.
- ✂ The other pizza refers to the pizza crust. Greek pizza is baked in a pan, unlike Italian pizza, which is baked directly on the bricks of a pizza oven. This Greek pizza has a thick, chewy crust and is usually oily; the ingredients do not have to be Greek. This type is typical of the restaurants owned by Greek immigrants (Wikipedia, 2006).

ADULT PREPARATION:

1. Mix together:
   a. 1 cup buttermilk dressing
   b. 1 stick softened butter
   c. ¼ teaspoon garlic powder

continued

46

Greek Pizza continued

2. Chop black olives on a cutting board and put them in a bowl.
3. Chop the green onions on a cutting board and put in a bowl.
4. Chop ham slices and put in a bowl.
5. Put shredded mozzarella cheese in a bowl.
6. Separate the halves of English muffins and put them on a plate.
7. Cover the baking sheet with aluminum foil.
8. Preheat the oven to 350°.

MATERIALS:
Aluminum foil
Globe
Spoons
Permanent marker

PROCEDURES:

The child will complete the following steps:
1. Find the state he or she lives in on the globe with the adult's assistance.
2. Find Greece on the globe with the adult's assistance. Note the distance between the two.
3. Wash hands.
4. Place half of an English muffin on a plate.
5. Use a spoon to put and spread the buttermilk dressing mixture on the English muffin.
6. Use a spoon to put olives, onions, and ham on the English muffin.
7. Top the pizza with shredded mozzarella cheese.

The adult will complete the following steps:
1. Place the finished Greek pizza on the foil baking sheet.
2. Use the permanent marker to write the child's name under their pizza.
3. Once the baking sheet is full, bake for approximately 10 minutes.

⊘ SAFETY PRECAUTIONS:

✂ Watch children closely when using small foods to prevent choking hazards.
✂ Always check for food allergies before beginning a cooking project.

Hawaiian Lei

AGES: 3-5

GROUP SIZE:

2–6 children

DEVELOPMENTAL GOALS:

✄ To develop an awareness of geography and culture

✄ To stimulate fine muscle control

LEARNING OBJECTIVE:

Using flower cutouts, yarn, and straws, the child will string a Hawaiian lei.

MATERIALS:

Flower pattern (Appendix A13)
Pen
Foam sheets (assorted colors)
Yarn
Ruler
Straws (bright colors)
Scissors
Masking tape
Bowls
Hole punch
Globe

DISCUSSION SUGGESTIONS:

✄ In Hawaii, leis are given and worn as gestures of love and welcome.

✄ They previously symbolized peace agreements between Hawaiian chiefs.

✄ They are made from native flowers, leaves, seeds, feathers, nutshells, and even animal bones and teeth.

✄ A lei is worn draped on the shoulders, hanging down in the front and back (The Lei Tradition, 2005).

ADULT PREPARATION:

1. Copy, trace, and cut out assorted colors of flowers from the foam sheets.

2. Cut yarn into 12" lengths.

3. Wrap one end of the yarn with masking tape to make an aglet (like the end of a shoelace) for easier stringing.

4. Cut straws into 1" lengths and place them in a bowl.

5. Tie a section of straw onto the end of yarn without the tape to ensure the pieces do not fall off as the child strings them.

6. Punch a hole in the flowers and place then in a bowl.

PROCEDURES:

The child will complete the following steps:

1. Find the state he or she lives in on the globe with the adult's assistance.

2. Find Hawaii on the globe with the adult's assistance. Note the distance between the two.

3. Select a piece of yarn.

4. String the yarn through the foam flower.

5. String the yarn through a piece of straw.

6. Continue alternating steps 4 and 5 until the lei is complete.

The adult will complete the following step:

1. Tie the ends of the lei together.

continued

Hawaiian Lei continued

VARIATIONS:

✂ Use long pipe cleaners in place of yarn. It is easier for younger children to string with a pipe cleaner.

✂ Precut flowers may be purchased from craft stores in place of using paper flowers.

✂ Children may also string tissue paper that they have torn into small pieces.

⚠ SAFETY PRECAUTION:

Supervise children closely when working with small objects, such as the cut straws, to prevent choking hazards.

EXPANSIONS:

✂ Play Hawaiian music while children dance with their leis.

✂ Eat pineapple for snack.

Homes

GROUP SIZE:

2–5 children

DEVELOPMENTAL GOALS:

✄ To explore homes in our communities

✄ To develop problem solving skills

LEARNING OBJECTIVE:

Using pictures of homes, wooden blocks, interlocking blocks, and wooden notched logs, the children will build a home together.

MATERIALS:

Family Letter 3 (Appendix B4)
Pictures of homes
Basket
Wooden blocks
Interlocking blocks
Wooden notched logs

DISCUSSION SUGGESTIONS:

✄ There are all kinds of homes.

✄ There are big homes, little homes, and apartment or town homes.

✄ Homes are made of many materials. Some are made of brick, stone, straw, tin, mud, or wood.

ADULT PREPARATION:

1. Send home a family letter requesting that each child bring in a picture of their house, apartment building, duplex, etc.

2. Put the pictures in a basket.

Homes continued

PROCEDURES:

The children will complete the following steps:

1. Sit in a circle or semicircle.
2. Take turns pulling the picture of their home out of the basket and sharing it with the group.
3. Once all pictures have been shared, put the pictures back in the basket.
4. Put the basket of pictures in the block area.
5. Select a picture from the basket and select the type of blocks desired for building. Choose from wooden blocks, interlocking blocks, or wooden notched logs.
6. Attempt to create the home with blocks.

BOOK SUGGESTION:

House and Homes by Ann Morris (New York: Lothrop, Lee & Shepard Books, 1992). This book introduces children to a variety of homes around the world using actual photographs.

EXPANSION:

Children may work together to create a house of their own design.

Ice Fishing

GROUP SIZE:

2 children

DEVELOPMENTAL GOALS:

✄ To develop awareness of the environment

✄ To coordinate muscles

LEARNING OBJECTIVE:

Using a dishpan with ice, a magnetic fishing pole, foam fish, and a small bucket, the children will take turns ice fishing.

MATERIALS:

Plastic dishpan
Water
Empty coffee can
Fish pattern
    (Appendix 14)
Pen
Foam sheets
Scissors
Metal paper clips
Magnetic wand
String
2' wooden dowel
Towel
Two chairs
Book about ice fishing
Small bucket

DISCUSSION SUGGESTIONS:

✄ People who ice fish use a sled to get equipment onto the ice.

✄ An ice auger drills a hole in the ice until open water can be seen.

✄ An ice chisel can help widen the hole. The hole should be no more than 12" wide.

✄ Fish must be a certain length to keep. Small fish must be released back into the water (Everything You Need to Know about Ice Fishing, n.d.)

ADULT PREPARATION:

1. Fill a plastic dishpan ⅔ full with water.

2. Set an empty coffee can in the center of the dishpan. Weigh the coffee can down by adding water to it, until it doesn't float. The coffee can needs to rise above the surface of the water.

3. Set the dishpan with the coffee can in the freezer overnight.

4. Using the fish pattern, copy, trace, and cut 10–20 fish out of the foam sheets.

continued

Ice Fishing continued

5. Attach a metal paper clip to each foam fish.

6. Tie one end of the magnetic wand to the string.

7. Tie the other end of the string to the two foot wooden dowel. This is now a fishing pole.

8. Once the water is frozen, remove the dishpan from the freezer.

9. Add warm water to the coffee can.

10. Once the warm water has loosened the coffee can, remove the can from the frozen water of the dish pan.

11. Place the foam fish into the hole in the ice.

12. Put a towel on the floor; set the dishpan on the towel.

13. Set two chairs near the dishpan.

PROCEDURES:

The child will complete the following steps:

1. Listen to a book read about ice fishing.

2. Sit in a chair.

3. Take turns using the fishing pole to dip the magnetic wand into the hole in the ice.

4. "Catch" the fish and remove them from the wand and place them in a small bucket.

NOTE:

A magnetic wand may be purchased at a school supply store or through a catalogue. If one is not available, a magnet tied to a string is sufficient.

BOOK SUGGESTION:

For four- and five-year-olds, read the storybook, *Kitaq* by Margaret Nicolei (Anchorage, AK: Alaska Northwest Books, 1998). Kitaq is a young Alaskan boy who goes ice fishing with his grandfather for the first time. This book may be paraphrased for younger children.

Independence Day

AGES: 3–5

GROUP SIZE:
2–3 children

DEVELOPMENTAL GOALS:
- ✄ To develop national identity
- ✄ To promote creativity

LEARNING OBJECTIVE:
Using a smock, sand filled socks, a box, black construction paper, florescent paint mixed with dish soap, and newspaper, the child will create a fireworks scene.

MATERIALS:
Measuring cup (1 cup)
Sand
Socks
Rubber bands
Florescent tempera paint
Foam plates
Dish soap
Tablespoon
Newspaper
Box (copy paper box works well)
Black construction paper
Smock

DISCUSSION SUGGESTIONS:
- ✄ Independence Day celebrates the birthday of the United States. It was founded on July 4, 1776, with the signing of the Declaration of Independence.
- ✄ Many towns have Fourth of July parades.
- ✄ Many people have picnics and gather to watch fireworks on Independence Day.

ADULT PREPARATION:
1. Pour 1 cup of sand into socks. Tie off the sock or seal it with a rubber band. Make one sock for each color of paint used.
2. Put different colors of florescent paint onto individual foam plates. Mix the paint with approximately 1–2 tablespoons of dish soap.
3. Lay newspaper on the floor.
4. Put a box on the newspaper.
5. Put black construction paper in the box.

PROCEDURES:
The child will complete the following steps:
1. Listen to a book about Independence Day.
2. Put on a smock.
3. Dip the sand sock into florescent paint.
4. Drop the sand sock into the box and then onto the black construction paper.
5. Repeat steps 2–3 with other colors, using a separate sock for each color.

NOTE:
Dropping the sand sock makes a starburst of paint on the black paper, simulating fireworks. Children may use the same paper to create a group project, or they may make an individual fireworks display.

BOOK SUGGESTION:
Independence Day by Helen Frost (Mankato, MN: Capstone Press, 2000). The history of Independence Day and the way we celebrate the holiday is explored in this book with colorful photographs.

54

Island

AGES: 3–5

GROUP SIZE:
2–4 children

DEVELOPMENTAL GOALS:
- ✄ To develop an understanding of geography
- ✄ To develop tactile senses

LEARNING OBJECTIVE:
Using a large tub or sensory table, sand, a bucket of water, a cup, smock, and plastic trees, the children will create an island.

MATERIALS:
Newspaper
Sand
Two large plastic containers
Cups
Water
Pie pans
Towel
Book about an island
Smock
Plastic trees

DISCUSSION SUGGESTIONS:

- ✄ An island is a body of land surrounded on all sides by water.
- ✄ People who want to get to an island have to take a boat, a plane, a ferry, or drive across a bridge.

ADULT PREPARATION:

1. Cover the table with newspaper.
2. Put sand in a large tub; place two cups in the sand.
3. Put water in the second tub.
4. Set the tub of sand, the tub of water, and the pie pans on the newspaper.
5. Place a towel nearby for spills.

PROCEDURES:

The children will complete the following steps:

1. Listen to a book read about an island.
2. Put on a smock.
3. Working in pairs, put a cup full of sand into a pile in the center of the pie pan.
4. Use the cup to place water around the pile, until the pile is completely surrounded by water like an island.
5. Push plastic trees into the island.

continued

Island continued

BOOK SUGGESTIONS:

✄ *An Island in the Sun* by Stella Blackstone (Cambridge, MA: Barefoot Books, 2002). A young man sails across the sea to an island noting everything he sees, saying the additional things he sees in the tradition of *This is the House that Jack Built.*

✄ *There Once Was a Puffin* by Florence Jaques (New York: North-South Books, Inc., 2003). A puffin lives alone on an island and has no one to play with.

Janitor

DISCUSSION SUGGESTIONS:

- ✂ Janitors take care of buildings such as schools, businesses, libraries, etc.
- ✂ They work on equipment when it breaks.
- ✂ A janitor may carry a phone, pager, or radio so they can be reached at all times.
- ✂ They have keys to most if not all the doors in a building.
- ✂ They may unlock the doors in the morning and lock them at night.
- ✂ Janitors use tools like hammers, nails, drills, mops, brooms, vacuum cleaners, and floor polishers.
- ✂ Many janitors work at night.
- ✂ Some janitors wear uniforms.

ADULT PREPARATION:

1. Fill the spray bottle with water.

PROCEDURES:

The child will complete the following steps:

1. Listen to a book about a janitor.
2. Use the spray bottle to spray tables or counters with water.
3. Use the wash cloth to wipe up the water.
4. Use the child-size broom and dust pan to sweep the floor.

NOTE:

If a small vacuum is also available, the child may vacuum the carpet.

BOOK SUGGESTIONS:

- ✂ *The Custodian from the Black Lagoon* by Mike Thaler (New York: Scholastic, Inc., 2001). The custodian at school is a scary person until a student actually meets him. This is a good book to also discuss the difference between fact and fantasy with children.
- ✂ *Night Shift Daddy* by Eileen Spinelli (New York: Hyperion Books for Children, 2000). A little girl's father works as a janitor at night. The book parallels each one's nighttime routine.

J

AGES: 3–5

GROUP SIZE:
2–4 children

DEVELOPMENTAL GOALS:

- ✂ To role play an occupation in our community
- ✂ To develop prosocial behaviors

LEARNING OBJECTIVE:

Using a spray bottle with water, a wash cloth, child-size broom, and a child-size dust pan, the child will enact the role of janitor.

MATERIALS:

Spray bottle
Water
Book about a janitor
Wash cloth
Child-size broom
Child-size dust pan

Japan's Origami

AGES: 4–5

GROUP SIZE:

2–6 children

DEVELOPMENTAL GOALS:

✄ To value and appreciate art forms from another culture

✄ To develop fine motor skills

LEARNING OBJECTIVE:

Using paper and markers, the child will create an origami dog.

MATERIALS:

Copy paper (various colors)
Ruler
Scissors
Globe
Markers

DISCUSSION SUGGESTIONS:

1. Origami is a Japanese art form. "In Japanese, 'ori' means fold and 'kami' means paper. People in Japan have enjoyed this art for hundreds of years" (LaFosse, 2002, p. 4).

2. Many different objects can be made with origami. Some people like to make animals such as cranes, fish, or dogs.

ADULT PREPARATION:

1. Cut various colors of copy paper into 5½" squares. Cut at least one for each child.

PROCEDURES:

The child will complete the following steps:

1. Find the state he or she lives in on the globe with the adult's assistance.

2. Find Japan on the globe with the adult's assistance. Note the distance between the two.

continued

58

Japan's Origami continued

3. Watch and repeat the following steps that an adult demonstrates:
   a. Fold the paper into a triangle by bringing opposite corners together.
   b. Smooth the fold flat.
   c. Take one of the corners on the fold and bend it down approximately 2–3 inches.
   d. Smooth this fold flat.
   e. Repeat steps c–d with the other corner on the main fold.
   f. This creates a dog.
4. Use markers to make facial features on the dog.

NOTES:

✄ Wrapping paper, magazines, candy wrappers, etc. may be used in place of copy paper.

✄ A paper cutter may be used in place of the scissors and ruler.

EXPANSION:

When children are ready for more difficult origami, refer to the *Kid's Guide to Origami* series written by Michael G. LaFosse (New York: PowerKids Press, 2002).

J

GROUP SIZE:

1 child

DEVELOPMENTAL GOALS:

✂ To role-play an occupation

✂ To enhance vocabulary

LEARNING OBJECTIVE:

Using a newspaper or magazine with pictures, glue, and a pencil, the child will dictate a story and create a byline.

MATERIALS:

Construction paper
Marker, pen, or pencil
Masking tape
Book about a journalist
Newspaper
Magazine
Scissors
Copy paper
Glue

Journalist

DISCUSSION SUGGESTIONS:

✂ A journalist is an author who writes articles for a newspaper or magazine.

✂ The journalist may also be called a reporter.

✂ A byline in a newspaper or magazine article lists the author's name.

ADULT PREPARATION:

1. Write *journalist* on a piece of construction paper.
2. Tape the paper to the wall or table.

PROCEDURES:

The child will complete the following steps:

1. Listen to a story read about a journalist.
2. Identify the author's byline in a newspaper or magazine with adult assistance.
3. Look through the newspaper or magazine and select a picture.

continued

Journalist continued

4. Remove the page from the newspaper or magazine with adult assistance.

5. Dictate a story about the picture to the adult.

6. Glue the story under or above the picture on the magazine or newspaper page.

7. Sign his or her name to the page, with adult assistance if needed, creating his or her own byline.

8. Listen to adult read story aloud.

BOOK SUGGESTION:

Newspaper by Catherine Anderson (Chicago: Heinemann Library, 2005). The process of creating a newspaper is illuminated through photographs. The procedure starts with the reporters who write the stories and ends with distribution.

Jungle

GROUP SIZE:

2–5 children

DEVELOPMENTAL GOALS:

- ✄ To appreciate animals in different environments
- ✄ To promote visual acuity

LEARNING OBJECTIVE:

Using jungle animal cutouts, a jungle animal tally sheet, binoculars, and a pencil, the child will identify and count animals.

MATERIALS:

Copy paper
Scissors
Crayons or markers
Jungle animal patterns
(Appendix A15–A19)
    Frog (Appendix A15)
    Green iguana
    (Appendix A16)
    Mandrill monkey
    (Appendix A17)
    Snake
    (Appendix A18)
    Toucan
    (Appendix A19)

DISCUSSION SUGGESTIONS:

- ✄ Frogs are reptiles.
  - ✄ They are also amphibians, which means they spend part of their life in and under water, and the rest of the time on land.
  - ✄ Frogs are nocturnal. They are active at night. During the day they rest on the underside of large leaves.
  - ✄ They eat mainly insects, catching them with long sticky tongues.
- ✄ The green iguana is a reptile.
  - ✄ It has a long tail and four long legs.
  - ✄ It eats leaves, flowers, fruit, and insects.
  - ✄ It has saw-like teeth.
  - ✄ Iguanas may grow to be 6' long.
- ✄ The mandrill monkey is large and ferocious.
  - ✄ It is the biggest monkey that lives on the ground, but it sleeps in the trees.
  - ✄ It has dark brown fur, a bright red nose, a blue snout, and a short stubby tail.
  - ✄ It eats mostly plants but also eats insects, lizards, and snakes.
- ✄ The snake is also a reptile.
  - ✄ It has scaly skin and a long narrow body.
  - ✄ The snake doesn't have eyelids, ear openings, or legs.
  - ✄ The largest snakes live in the jungle or rainforest.
- ✄ The toucan is a bird.
  - ✄ It is a poor flyer and prefers to hop around trees.
  - ✄ It roosts in holes and trees.
  - ✄ The toucan makes a croaking call that sounds like RRRRRK.
  - ✄ It eats mostly fruit, bird eggs, and tree frogs.

(Enchanted Learning, n.d)

NOTE:

More information about jungle animals may be found at http://www.enchantedlearning.com

continued

Jungle continued

ADULT PREPARATION:

1. Copy, cut out, and color 4–6 of each jungle animal pattern.
2. Tape the animals around the classroom.
3. Make one copy of the jungle animal tally sheet for each child.

PROCEDURES:

The child will complete the following steps:

1. Use the binoculars to find the jungle animals throughout the classroom.
2. When an animal is found, identify the animal and make a mark in the appropriate column of the jungle animal tally sheet.
3. When all animals are found, count the number of each type of animal.

NOTE:

Binoculars may be made by hot gluing two toilet tissue tubes together. Holes may be punched in the outside of each tube and then string tied to each hole, creating a neck strap.

EXPANSION:

Graph the number of animals found.

MATERIALS:

Toy binoculars
Jungle animal
  tally sheet
  (Appendix A20)
Pencil

Kenya's Soccer

AGES: 3–5

GROUP SIZE:
2–3 children

DEVELOPMENTAL GOALS:
- ✂ To value and appreciate people across cultures
- ✂ To develop large muscles

LEARNING OBJECTIVE:
Using child-size soccer goals and balls, the children will play soccer.

MATERIALS:
Child-size soccer goals
Globe
Soccer balls

DISCUSSION SUGGESTIONS:
- ✂ One of the favorite sports in Kenya is soccer.
- ✂ In Kenya, soccer is called football.
- ✂ Kenya has a national soccer team (Saffer, 2002).

ADULT PREPARATION:
1. Set up two child-size soccer goals. Put one at each end of a grassy area.

PROCEDURES:
The child will complete the following steps:
1. Find the state he or she lives in on the globe with the adult's assistance.
2. Find Kenya on the globe with the adult's assistance. Note the distance between the two.
3. Take turns kicking the soccer balls into the goals.

continued

64

Kenya's Soccer continued

4. Divide into two teams. Select a goal for each team.
5. Use only one soccer ball as the team members try to kick the ball into their goal.

BOOK SUGGESTION:

For more information on soccer read *Soccer: Skills* by Barbara Bonney (Vero Beach, FL: The Rourke Press, Inc., 1997).

K

AGES: 2–5

GROUP SIZE:

2–15 children

DEVELOPMENTAL GOALS:

- To show respect for others
- To encourage emotional development

LEARNING OBJECTIVE:

Using a song board, the children will sing a kindness song.

MATERIALS:

Markers, crayons, or colored pencils
Poster board
Copy paper
Scissors
Kindness patterns (Appendix A21–24)
Child holding door open for another (Appendix A21)
Child sharing toys with another (Appendix A22)
Child hanging up his coat (Appendix A23)
Child giving another child a hug (Appendix A24)
Rubber cement
Book about being kind

Kindness

DISCUSSION SUGGESTIONS:

- To be kind means you consider other people.
- You need to try to do nice things for others.
- Being kind means using your good manners with others.
- People should treat others the way they want to be treated.
- "What nice things do you want people to do for you?" Those are the things you should do for others.

ADULT PREPARATION:

1. Write the words to the song *KINDNESS* on a poster board.
2. Copy, color, and cut out the kindness patterns; use rubber cement to glue them near the corners of the poster board.

PROCEDURES:

The children will complete the following steps:

1. Listen to book read about being kind.
2. Using the song board, the child will sing the following song to the tune of *Mickey Mouse*.

KINDNESS

K-I-N-D-N-E-S-S spells kindness.
Hold the door,
Share your toys,
Hang up a coat, or give a hug.
K-I-N-D-N-E-S-S spells kindness.

BOOK SUGGESTIONS:

- *Being Kind* by Janine Amos (Milwaukee, WI: Gareth Stevens Publishing, 2002). Two short vignettes are presented where children notice another's discomfort and then act with kindness.
- *The Child's World of Kindness* by Jane Moncure (Chanhassen, MN: Child's World, Inc., 1997). Kindness is demonstrated in this text.

EXPANSION:

Children brainstorm other ways to be kind. Adult writes suggestions down, then the ideas are incorporated into the kindness song.

Liberty Bell

DISCUSSION SUGGESTIONS:

✄ The Liberty Bell was made for the Pennsylvania Assembly in 1752.

✄ Bells were used to proclaim news, announce meetings, and warn of danger.

✄ The Liberty Bell cracked in 1835. The first chief justice of the Supreme Court was John Marshall. The bell was rung upon his death and split (Sakurai, 1996).

✄ The Liberty Bell weighs 2,080 pounds. It is 12' around and is 7½' tall (Liberty Bell Museum, 2006).

ADULT PREPARATION:

1. Copy, cut out, and color two copies of the Liberty Bell pattern.
2. Use rubber cement to glue both copies on tag board or poster board.
3. When dry, cut out the reinforced Liberty Bell cutouts.
4. Cut one bell into puzzle pieces.
5. Store puzzle pieces and intact bell in a resealable plastic bag.

PROCEDURES:

The child will complete the following steps:

1. Listen to a story about the Liberty Bell.
2. Remove bell and puzzle pieces from storage bag.
3. Place puzzle pieces together on top of intact bell.

NOTE:

With younger children cut fewer and larger pieces. Older children may not need the intact bell to use as a reference.

BOOK SUGGESTION:

The Liberty Bell by Lloyd G. Douglas (New York: Rosen Book Works, Inc., 2003). The Liberty Bell is introduced through simple text and photographs.

AGES: 3–5

GROUP SIZE:
2–3 children

DEVELOPMENTAL GOALS:

✄ To develop a sense of history

✄ To stimulate eye-hand coordination

LEARNING OBJECTIVE:
Using a Liberty Bell cutout and Liberty Bell pieces, the child will put a puzzle together.

MATERIALS:
Copy paper
Markers, crayons, or colored pencils
Scissors
Liberty Bell pattern (Appendix A25)
Rubber cement
Tag board or poster board
Resealable plastic bag
Book about the Liberty Bell

L

AGES: 3–5

GROUP SIZE:

2–3 children

DEVELOPMENTAL GOALS:

- ✄ To role-play an occupation
- ✄ To engage in social interactions

LEARNING OBJECTIVE:

Using books, a book shelf or crate, a notebook, index cards, sticky notepad, a stamp, and stamp pad, the children will take turns playing librarian.

MATERIALS:

Children's books
Book shelf or crate
Index cards
Pen or pencil
Book about a librarian
Large sheet of paper
Marker
Small basket
Stamp
Stamp pad
Sticky notepad

Librarian

DISCUSSION SUGGESTIONS:

- ✄ The librarian helps people find and check out books.
- ✄ The librarian orders all the books in the library.
- ✄ He or she makes sure all the books, magazines, movies, and music are in their proper place.
- ✄ The librarian can schedule special events at the library.
- ✄ He or she can help a person look up any information needed.

ADULT PREPARATION:

1. Write the title of each book on individual index cards and place the cards in the appropriate book.
2. Put the books on a shelf or in a crate.

PROCEDURES:

The children will complete the following steps:

1. Listen to book read about a librarian.
2. Answer the adult's question, "What do librarians do?"
3. Watch as the adult writes the responses on a large sheet of paper with a marker.

continued

Librarian continued

4. Take turns acting out the roles of librarian and customer.
5. The customer will select a book to check out and will take it to the librarian.
6. The librarian will take the index card out of the book and place the card in the basket.
7. The librarian will stamp a sticky note and will place it in the inside of the book.
8. Children may switch roles and repeat steps 4–7.

BOOK SUGGESTION:

Ms. Davison, Our Librarian by Alice K. Flanagan (New York: Children's Press, 1996). Ms. Davison is a librarian who works in the neighborhood where she grew up.

Magician

AGES: 3–5

GROUP SIZE:
2–3 children

DEVELOPMENTAL GOALS:
- ✄ To appreciate different occupations
- ✄ To practice role-playing

LEARNING OBJECTIVE:
Using a black top hat, stuffed toy rabbit, small plastic flower, magic wand, and a handkerchief, the children will take turns acting as a magician.

MATERIALS:
Black spray paint
12" wooden dowel
Masking tape
Permanent marker
Construction paper
Small plastic flower
Black top hat
Stuffed toy rabbit
Handkerchief
Book about a magician

DISCUSSION SUGGESTIONS:
- ✄ Magicians perform tricks of magic.
- ✄ They do not tell how they do their tricks.
- ✄ One way to learn magic tricks is from books.
- ✄ Magicians perform magic either as a hobby or as a job.

ADULT PREPARATION:
1. Spray paint a 12" wooden dowel black.
2. When the dowel is dry, tape a ring of masking tape on each end of the dowel to create a magic wand.
3. Write *magician* on a piece of construction paper; tape it to the wall or table.
4. Put a small plastic flower in the bottom of the hat.
5. Put a stuffed toy rabbit in the hat.
6. Place handkerchief beside the hat.

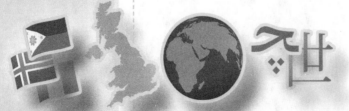

continued

Magician continued

PROCEDURES:

The children will complete the following steps:

1. Look at the word taped to the wall. Listen as the adult says the word is "magician."
2. Listen to the adult explain that magicians do magic tricks.
3. Listen to a book read about a magician.
4. Watch the adult demonstrate:

    a. How they cover the top hat with a handkerchief.

    b. Wave the magic wand above the hat and say, "Abracadabra."

    c. Take the handkerchief off the hat and pull the rabbit out of the hat.

    d. Cover the top hat with a handkerchief.

    e. Wave the magic wand about the hat and say, "Abracadabra."

    f. Take the handkerchief off the hat and pull the flower out of the hat.

5. Take turns reenacting step 4.

NOTE:

A black top hat may be made from black construction paper:

1. Staple the paper into a cylinder.
2. Cut 1" slashes at the top of the cylinder.
3. Cut a circle 4" larger than the diameter of the cylinder.
4. Fold the slashes at the top of the cylinder and staple the folds to the circle.

BOOK SUGGESTION:

Abiyoyo by Pete Seeger (New York: Simon & Schuster, 1994). A boy's father is a magician and can make things disappear. He saves the town by making a monster disappear.

Mapping

AGES: 4–5

GROUP SIZE:

2–5 children

DEVELOPMENTAL GOALS:

✄ To develop pre-mapping skills

✄ To develop visual discrimination

LEARNING OBJECTIVE:

Using paper, crayons, and the book and materials from *The Three Little Pigs*, the children will create a 3-D and 2-D map.

MATERIALS:

Bags (3)
Straw
Sticks
Interlocking blocks
A *Three Little Pigs* book
Child-size scissors
Gray or black
 construction paper
Step stool
Blank paper
Crayons

DISCUSSION SUGGESTIONS:

✄ Maps help people find specific places.

✄ There are many kinds of maps: road maps, city, state, or country maps, maps of rooms and schools, park maps, etc.

✄ Maps have special drawing or symbols on them to tell us where things such as roads, trails, rest stops, parks, and lakes are located.

ADULT PREPARATION:

1. Clear an area on the floor to build a 3-D map.

2. Put straw in one bag, sticks in a second bag, and interlocking blocks in a third bag.

PROCEDURES:

The children will complete the following steps:

1. Listen to the story of *The Three Little Pigs*.

2. Divide the group into thirds.

3. One group builds a house of straw.

4. The second group builds a house of sticks.

5. The third group builds a house of bricks (interlocking blocks).

continued

6. The fourth group cuts gray or black construction paper into strips and lays them down for roads between the houses.

7. Take turns standing on a step stool to get an aerial perspective of the area with house and roads.

8. Listen to the adult explain that maps help show us where things are.

9. Select a sheet of blank paper and crayons.

10. Create a map by drawing the three houses with the roads between the houses.

Note: This activity was provided by Kathy Gosman of Loganville, Georgia.

BOOK SUGGESTIONS:

✂ *The Three Little Pigs* by Harriet Ziefert (New York: Viking, 1995). This easy-to-read book has simple illustrations of the pigs' homes.

✂ *The Three Little Pigs* by James Marshall (New York: Dial Books for Young Readers, 1989). The homes in this book are more elaborate, such as having the stick house up on stilts.

EXPANSIONS:

✂ Share different maps with children, such as the classroom evacuation map, park maps, road maps, state, or country maps.

✂ Make different kinds of maps with the children, such as a map of objects or a room. *Maps and Globes* by Sabrina Crewe (New York: Children's Press, 1996) helps with a step-by-step process for teaching children to use and understand maps.

Mexican Piñata

DISCUSSION SUGGESTIONS:

✂ The piñata is used as a fun game in Mexico, during *Posadoas*, which is the traditional procession to begin the start of the Christmas season, and at birthday parties.

✂ Piñatas are found in all shapes and sizes. They may be filled with both candy and fruit.

✂ At Christmas time in Mexico, the piñata may be stuffed with things such as wrapped candy, guavas, oranges, or sugar cane (Devlin, 1999).

ADULT PREPARATION:

1. Write children's names on individual resealable plastic bags with a permanent marker.
2. Put an equal amount of individually wrapped candy in each bag; seal the bags.
3. Put the bags of candy inside the piñata.
4. Tie one end of the heavy string to the piñata.
5. Tie the other end of the heavy string to a tree branch outside. Make sure the piñata is within the children's reach.
6. Set a row of chairs outside, out of the way of the piñata. Put out the number of chairs equal to the number of children.

PROCEDURES:

The children will complete the following steps:
1. Sit in a chair.
2. Find the state he or she lives in on the globe with the adult's assistance.
3. Find Mexico on the globe with the adult's assistance. Note the distance between the two.
4. Listen to the adult explain that piñatas are a way to celebrate in Mexico.
5. Take turns hitting the piñata one or two times with a stick or bat.
6. Continue taking turns until the piñata breaks and the bags of candy fall to the ground.
7. Children search for the bag of candy with their name.

continued

Mexican Piñata continued

NOTES:

✂ Putting the candy in a labeled resealable plastic bag helps children to recognize their name and ensures that all children receive an equal amount of candy.

✂ If a piñata is not available, use a large paper grocery bag that children may decorate with tissue paper.

✂ If a piñata stick is not available, use the heavy empty tube from a roll of laminating film or a plastic bat.

✂ Young children do not need to be blindfolded. Many children have difficulty hitting the piñata even when they are not blindfolded.

✂ If parents oppose the use of candy, substitute it with healthy snacks, such as boxed raisins, granola bars, or small toys.

⚠ SAFETY PRECAUTIONS:

✂ Supervise children closely so no one gets hurt when the piñata stick is being swung. Having children sit in a chair while they wait their turn ensures they will be safely out of the way of the bat being swung.

✂ Avoid using hard candies or candy with nuts. Watch children closely when eating candy to prevent choking hazards.

BOOK SUGGESTION:

Hooray! A Piñata! by Elisa Kleven (New York: Dutton Children's Books, 1996). Clara wants a piñata for her birthday. She picks out a small dog piñata, but when she becomes attached to it, she doesn't want to break it. Her friend, Samson, comes to her rescue.

N

Native Americans' Pueblo Village

AGES: 3–5

DEVELOPMENTAL GOALS:

- ✂ To develop a sense of history
- ✂ To promote problem solving

LEARNING OBJECTIVE:

Using wooden blocks, wooden notched logs, and a picture of a Pueblo village, the children will recreate the village.

MATERIALS:

Picture of a Pueblo village
Wooden blocks
Wooden notched logs

DISCUSSION SUGGESTIONS:

- ✂ The Native Americans' Pueblo villages were apartment-like dwellings built into cliffs or on top of mesas. A mesa is a high flat area that has steep sides (Bowen, 2003).
- ✂ These homes were box shaped, built in rows, and built with adobe (clay) or sandstone.
- ✂ Some Pueblo villages had homes that were built on top of each other. This style of building saved space and protected the Pueblos from their enemies.
- ✂ Sometimes the homes were stacked four to five houses high. People used ladders to climb up to their homes (Ross, 1999).

ADULT PREPARATION:

1. Locate a picture of a Native America Pueblo village either from the Internet or in a book.
2. Display the picture in the block area.
3. Set out wooden blocks and wooden notched logs.

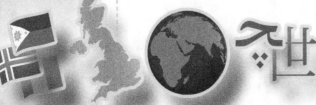

continued

Native Americans' Pueblo Village continued

PROCEDURES:

The child will complete the following steps:

1. Look at the picture of the Pueblo village.

2. Use the wooden blocks to make the connected box-shaped homes.

3. Use the wooden notched logs to make the ladders to the different levels.

BOOK SUGGESTION:

The Pueblo Indians by Pamela Ross (Mankato, MN: Bridgestone Books, 1999). This book shows color photographs of a Pueblo village. The text is informative but would need to be paraphrased for younger children. It also contains a recipe for making adobe bricks.

Netherlands' Wooden Shoes

AGES: 2–5

GROUP SIZE:

2–5 children

DEVELOPMENTAL GOALS:

✂ To appreciate the culture of others

✂ To stimulate eye-hand coordination

LEARNING OBJECTIVE:

Using a wooden shoe cutout and a small stencil with flowers or scrolls, the children will decorate the cutout.

MATERIALS:

Copy paper
Wooden shoe pattern
(Appendix 26)
Scissors
Pencil
Construction paper
Tempera paint
Foam plate
Dish soap
Spoon
Paper towel
Masking tape
Small stencil with
flowers or scrolls
Smock
Small sponge

DISCUSSION SUGGESTIONS:

✂ Children of the Netherlands set out wooden shoes at Christmastime for St. Nicholas to fill, much like children of the United States put out stockings for Santa Claus.

✂ Wooden shoes are worn by farmers in the Netherlands when walking through dirt and mud.

ADULT PREPARATION:

1. Copy the wooden shoe pattern.
2. Use the pattern to make cutouts from construction paper.
3. Pour tempera paint into the foam plate; mix with approximately a spoonful of dish soap.
4. Fold paper towel to fit plate and lay it on top of the paint.
5. Flip paper towel over. This creates a paint blotter.
6. Use masking tape to position the stencil on the wooden shoe cutout.

PROCEDURES:

The children will complete the following steps:

1. Wearing a smock, dip the small sponge onto the paint blotter.
2. Press the sponge on the stencil creating the design.
3. Repeat steps 1–2 using other colors if desired.
4. Remove stencil and tape from cutout.

NOTE:

Masking tape should be removed immediately to prevent the cutout from tearing.

VARIATION:

Allow the children to use their own creativity to decorate the shoe in place of using stencils.

Nurse

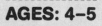

DISCUSSION SUGGESTIONS:

✂ A nurse has a job where they work in a doctor's office, hospital, or nursing home; some nurses go to the patient's home.

✂ Nurses can take temperature, blood pressure, measure height and weight, give medicine and shots, and many other things.

✂ Some nurses help doctors in surgery.

ADULT PREPARATION:

1. Write children's names on individual sheets of paper.

2. Create a nurse's office by laying the stethoscope, blood pressure cuff, clipboard, and pen or pencil on a table. Place the bathroom scale on the floor near the table.

PROCEDURES:

The children will complete the following steps:

1. Listen to book read about a nurse.

2. Answer the adult's question, "What does a nurse do?"

continued

AGES: 4–5

GROUP SIZE:
2 children

DEVELOPMENTAL GOALS:

✂ To develop awareness of different occupations

✂ To practice various roles

LEARNING OBJECTIVE:
Using a stethoscope, blood pressure cuff, clipboard, and paper, the children will take turns pretending to be a nurse.

MATERIALS:
Pen or pencil
Paper
Book about a nurse
Stethoscope
Blood pressure cuff
Clipboard
Bathroom scale
Alcohol wipes, or cotton balls and rubbing alcohol

Nurse continued

3. Assign roles of nurse and patient.
4. The nurse will wear the stethoscope around their neck.
5. The patient will select the paper with their name and give it to the nurse.
6. The nurse will complete the following:
   a. Put the paper on the clipboard.
   b. Ask the patient to step on the scale.
   c. Identify the nearest number on the scale and write the patient's weight on the paper on the clipboard.
   d. Take the patient's blood pressure, using the blood pressure cuff and stethoscope.
   e. Write a number for blood pressure in the chart.
   f. Ask the patient why they came to the doctor.

The adult will complete the following steps:

1. Using an alcohol wipe, or cotton ball and rubbing alcohol, wipe down the ear pieces.
2. Invite the children to switch roles.

BOOK SUGGESTION:

A Day in the Life of a Nurse by Connie Fluet (Mankato, MN: Capstone Press, 2005). A nurse is photographed as he performs his duties.

Observatory

AGES: 3–5

GROUP SIZE:
4–6 children

DEVELOPMENTAL GOALS:

✂ To develop an appreciation of outer space

✂ To promote social development through taking turns

LEARNING OBJECTIVE:

Using glow-in-the-dark stars, a toy telescope, and a battery-operated lantern, lamp, or flashlight, the children will pretend to be in an observatory.

MATERIALS:

Glow-in-the-dark stars
Masking tape
Toy telescope
Book about stars
Battery operated lantern, lamp, or flashlight

DISCUSSION SUGGESTIONS:

✂ An observatory is a special building where people observe or watch the stars, planets, and weather.

✂ Scientists study objects in the sky in an observatory.

✂ They use very powerful telescopes to see the stars, planets, and comets in space.

ADULT PREPARATION:

1. Use masking tape to place glow-in-the-dark stars on the ceiling and walls.

2. Put the toy telescope on a stand or table, so the telescope is at the children's eye level.

continued

Observatory continued

PROCEDURES:

The children will complete the following steps:

1. Listen to the adult read a book about looking at stars.
2. Turn off the lights in the classroom.
3. If the room does not have natural light, use a battery-operated lantern, lamp, or flashlight to illuminate part of the room. However, it must be dark enough to see the stars glow.
4. Take turns looking through the telescope at the stars.
5. Pick out a star and name it after him or her.

NOTE:

If a toy telescope is not available, make handheld telescopes with empty paper towel or gift wrap tubes. Place blue plastic wrap over the end of the tube and hold it in place with a rubber band.

BOOK SUGGESTION:

Stars by Melanie Mitchell (Minneapolis, MN: Lerner Publications Company, 2004). This easy-to-read book shows photographs of stars.

82

Ocean

DISCUSSION SUGGESTIONS:

- ✀ The ocean is a large body of salt water.
- ✀ Another word for ocean is sea.
- ✀ The ocean covers approximately 70% of the earth (University of Delaware, n.d.).
- ✀ The ocean water moves constantly. The wind, the earth's rotation, and the water's temperature all affect the way the water moves (Feldman & Gradwohl, n.d.).

ADULT PREPARATION:

1. Remove the labels from the clear soda or water bottles. Remove and save the tops.
2. Add water to the child-size pitcher.
3. Put cooking oil in a bowl.

PROCEDURES:

The child will complete the following steps:

1. Listen to a book about oceans.
2. Look at the globe. Note that the large blue areas are oceans. Listen to the adult explain that 70% of the earth is covered with oceans.
3. Wearing a smock, place the funnel in the clear bottle.
4. Use the child-size pitcher to fill the bottle ⅔ full, with adult assistance if necessary.
5. Add several drops of blue or green food coloring to the bottle.
6. With adult assistance secure the lid on the bottle and shake the bottle to mix the coloring with the water.
7. Remove the lid and replace the funnel.
8. Add several tablespoons of oil to the bottle, with adult assistance if necessary.
9. Remove the funnel.
10. Secure the lid on the bottle with adult assistance.
11. Lay the bottle on its side and rock it from lid to base creating waves.
12. Allow the bottle to sit still to see the waves settle.

continued

Ages: 2½–5

GROUP SIZE:
2–5 children

DEVELOPMENTAL GOALS:
- ✀ To appreciate geography
- ✀ To develop an awareness of nature

LEARNING OBJECTIVE:
Using a 16–20 ounce clear soda or water bottle with lid, water, blue and green food coloring, a funnel, cooking oil, and a smock, the child will create the waves of an ocean.

MATERIALS:
16–20 ounce clear soda or water bottle with lid
Water
Child-size pitcher
Cooking oil
Bowl
Book about oceans
Globe
Smock
Funnel
Blue and green food coloring
Tablespoon

Ocean continued

BOOK SUGGESTIONS:

✂ *What are Oceans?* by Lisa Trumbauer (Mankato, MN: Capstone Press, 2002). Color photographs accompany the simple text in this book about oceans.

✂ *Exploring the Deep, Dark Sea* by Gail Gibbons (New York: Little, Brown & Company, 1999). Many facts are presented and sea creatures are labeled in this text.

NOTE:

The adult may hot glue the cap to the bottle to prevent children from opening the bottle.

Olympics

AGES: 3–5

GROUP SIZE:
8–20 children

DEVELOPMENTAL GOALS:
- ✂ To develop a global view
- ✂ To develop large muscles

LEARNING OBJECTIVE:
Using rhythmic ribbons, CD player with a musical CD, a ball with minimal bounce or a bean bag, and a balance beam, children will take turns participating in Olympic events.

MATERIALS:
Plunger
White, red, yellow, green, black, and blue tempera paint
Large white construction paper
Spring clothespins
Masking tape
House paint brush
White chalk
Rhythmic ribbons

DISCUSSION SUGGESTIONS:

- ✂ The first Olympics were held approximately 3,000 years ago.
- ✂ The Olympics are held every four years.
- ✂ There are separate winter and summer games.
- ✂ More countries send athletes to the summer games. Sports such as volleyball, swimming, tennis, and track are played in the summer.
- ✂ During the winter games, people ski, ice skate, bob sled, and play ice hockey. Some countries do not have these sports because of their warm weather (Middleton, 2003).

ADULT PREPARATION:

1. Create the Olympic ring logo by using a plunger and dipping it into paint, then pressing it onto a large sheet of paper.
2. To create the logo make 5 rings. The top 3 rings are blue, black, and red (from left to right). The 2 bottom rings are yellow and green (From left to right).
3. When the Olympic logo dries, hang it on a fence with clothespins or masking tape. If unable to use a fence, attach the logo to trees or chairs.

continued

85

Olympics continued

MATERIALS:

CD player with a
musical CD
Balance beam, railroad
ties, or 6' board that
is 4"–6" wide
Book about the
Olympics
Ball with minimal
bounce or bean bag

4. Divide the outdoor area into centers where the children will participate in the following events:

   a. Long jump

   b. Rhythmic ribbons

   c. Shot put

   d. Balance beam

5. To create the long jump, draw a line in the grass with white tempera paint and a house paint brush.

6. Set aside a large area for rhythmic ribbons. This may be done on concrete. Segregate this area by drawing a large square with chalk. This should be near an outlet, or set up a battery operated CD player, so children may use music in their routines.

7. For shot put, draw a circle in the grass with white tempera paint.

8. Set up a balance beam by using a commercial one, or set out a 6' board that is 4"–6" in width. Some playgrounds have railroad ties to hold in mulch; these ties may be used as the balance beam.

9. If white tempera paint is used, make sure all paint is dry before use.

PROCEDURES:

The children will complete the following steps:

1. Listen to the adult read a book about the Olympics.

2. Watch the adult demonstrate how to do the long jump, the shot put, balance beam, and how to use the rhythmic ribbons.

3. Take turns at the different stations.

4. While at the long jump, take turns standing with their toes on the line and then jumping forward, landing with both feet together.

5. At the rhythmic ribbon station, dance to music while twirling and waving their ribbons.

6. Take turns throwing the shot put (ball with minimal bounce, or bean bag) by holding it with one hand, placing that hand near the shoulder, and then shooting that arm upward and forward as they release the ball.

7. Take turns walking forward across the balance beam. As their skill level increases, the child may walk across the beam sideways or backwards. The adult may need to hold a child's hand as they cross until the skill or confidence level increases.

continued

Olympics continued

NOTES:

- ✄ If white tempera paint is used on the playground, make sure to notify the director and receive permission. It does wash away.
- ✄ If available, spray chalk may be used in place of white tempera paint.
- ✄ Children may be divided into groups that rotate to the various stations together, or they may have free choice to try the different events.
- ✄ If commercial rhythmic ribbons are not available, they can be made by stapling a 6′ length of wide ribbon to a wooden paint-stirrer stick.

BOOK SUGGESTION:

Read *Olympics!* by Barbara G. Hennessy (New York: Penguin Group, 1996). This book presents a brief synopsis of the Olympics from the preparation to the events.

P

GROUP SIZE:

2–3 children

DEVELOPMENTAL GOALS:

✄ To develop an awareness of occupations in our community

✄ To promote social development through socio-dramatic play

LEARNING OBJECTIVE:

Using a police hat, hairdryer without a cord, small notepad, pen or pencil, box, and plastic plate, the children will role-play police officer and driver.

MATERIALS:

Blue copy paper
Scissors
Police hat pattern
(Appendix A27)
Construction paper
Ruler
Stapler and staples
Large box

Police Officer

DISCUSSION SUGGESTIONS:

✄ Being a police officer is a job.

✄ A police officer has to go through special training.

continued

Police Officer continued

❧ Some police officers drive cars, ride bicycles, or ride motorcycles as they work. Others simply walk "their beat." The beat is the area the officer patrols.

❧ Police officers write people a ticket for bad driving, driving too fast, not wearing a seat belt, and causing accidents, among other things.

❧ Police officers also help direct traffic, help people solve arguments, and are here to serve and protect.

MATERIALS:
Box cutter
Plastic or paper plate
Hairdryer without
   a cord
Small notepad
Pen or pencil

ADULT PREPARATION:

1. Copy and cut out a police hat pattern for each child on blue copy paper.
2. Cut construction paper into 3" strips.
3. Staple strips together to fit around each child's head, making individual hat bands.
4. Staple the police hat cut-out on the hat band.
5. Create a car by cutting a door in a box large enough for a child to sit in.
6. Place a plastic or paper plate in the box for a child to use as a steering wheel.

PROCEDURES:

The children will complete the following steps:

1. Listen to a book about a police officer.
2. Discuss different tasks that a police officer must do.
3. Assign roles of police officer and driver.
4. The driver will take their place in the box and pretend to drive a car.
5. The police officer will put on their hat and hold their radar gun (hairdryer without the cord) towards the car.
6. The police officer will:

   a. Ask the driver to pull over.

   b. Set the radar gun down and tell the driver that they were speeding.

   c. Write a ticket in the small notepad and give the ticket to the driver.

7. Switch roles and repeat sets 3–6.

continued

Police Officer continued

BOOK SUGGESTION:

A Day in the Life of a Police Officer by Heather Adamson (Mankato, MN: Capstone Press, 2004). Photographs of a police officer are shown as he performs his various duties throughout the day.

EXPANSIONS:

✄ Change the scenario and have the police officer issue a ticket because the driver isn't wearing a seatbelt or because a child is not in a car seat.

✄ Practice dialing 911 for police help. Children must realize this number is only called in the event of an emergency.

Postal Worker

DISCUSSION SUGGESTIONS:

✼ A postal worker may collect the mail from mailboxes. She collects from big mailboxes that stand on the curbs or small mailboxes at people's homes.

✼ Different postal workers may sort the mail, load it on trucks or cars, and deliver the mail.

✼ Other postal workers may help people who come into the post office by selling stamps, envelopes, postcards, or weighing and mailing boxes.

✼ A postal worker must deliver the mail in all kinds of weather.

✼ Some postal workers walk around neighborhoods to deliver the mail.

✼ Other postal workers drive up to people's mail boxes on the curb to deliver the mail.

ADULT PREPARATION:

1. Write *letters* and *packages* on individual index cards.
2. Tape one index card to each laundry basket.
3. Write *Post Office* on a piece of construction paper and tape it to the wall or table.

PROCEDURES:

The children will complete the following steps:

1. Listen to a book about postal workers.
2. Assign roles of customer and postal worker.
3. Give play money to customer.
4. The customer will bring boxes or envelopes (junk mail) to the postal worker.
5. The postal worker will:
   a. Sell stamps (stickers).
   b. Weigh packages on the balance scale.
   c. Sort mail into different baskets. One basket for letters, the other basket for packages.
6. Switch roles and repeat steps 2–5.

AGES: 3–5

GROUP SIZE:
2–3 children

DEVELOPMENTAL GOALS:

✼ To acquire an awareness of community helpers

✼ To practice role-playing

LEARNING OBJECTIVE:

Using stickers for stamps, junk mail, shoe boxes with lids, labeled laundry baskets, cash register, play money, and a balance scale, the children will role-play postal worker and customer.

MATERIALS:

Marker
Index cards
Masking tape
Construction paper
Book about postal workers
Play money
Cash register
Shoe boxes with lids
Junk mail
Stickers
Balance scale
Two laundry baskets

continued

Postal Worker continued

BOOK SUGGESTIONS:

✄ *Postal Workers* by Paulette Bourgeois (Buffalo, NY: Kids Can Press, 1999). The author of the *Franklin* series follows Gordon's birthday card to Grandma. The duties of postal workers and the process letters go through are examined.

Preserving Personal History

AGES: 3–5

GROUP SIZE:
3–5 children when spreading glue on the shoes; 1 child when covering the shoe with gold spray paint

DEVELOPMENTAL GOALS:
- ✂ To develop a positive self-image
- ✂ To follow directions

LEARNING OBJECTIVE:
Using child's shoe, school glue, large brush, gold spray paint, and smock, the child will make a gift for their mother or significant female.

MATERIALS:
Family Letter 4
  (Appendix B5)
Child's shoe they have
  outgrown
Permanent marker
Wax paper
Tray
Cooking spray
School glue
Bowl

DISCUSSION SUGGESTIONS:

- ✂ Preserving personal history is a way to keep something that is important to a person.
- ✂ Taking pictures, writing in a journal, and preserving treasures from childhood help a person remember their past.
- ✂ When people get older, it is important to remember how they were when they were younger.

ADULT PREPARATION:

1. Copy family letter and send home with child requesting a shoe that the child has outgrown.
2. Write child's name on the bottom of the shoe with permanent marker.
3. Place wax paper on tray.
4. Spray bottom of the shoe with cooking spray.
5. Pour school glue into a bowl.

continued

Preserving Personal History continued

PROCEDURES:

The child will complete the following steps:

1. Put on smock.
2. Use the paint brush to cover shoe with glue on both the outside and the inside.
3. Repeat steps 1–2 for three or four days, until the shoe has dried and has hardened.

Adult will complete the following steps:

1. Check shoe for globs of glue. Smooth these areas with a brush.
2. Take shoe outside or to a well ventilated area.
3. Put shoe on newspaper.

Child will complete the following steps:

1. Put on smock.
2. Assist adult in spraying the shoe gold.
3. Leave shoe in well-ventilated area to dry.

NOTE:

Spraying the bottom of the shoe with cooking spray prevents it from sticking to the wax paper.

EXPANSION:

Take a picture of the child so they may have a keepsake of how they looked when they preserved his or her shoe. Make sure to have a copy of a permission form to be photographed on file for each child (see Appendix B2).

94

Qatar's Camel Racing

AGES: 3–5

GROUP SIZE:
4–10 children

DEVELOPMENTAL GOALS:
- To develop an appreciation for the culture of others
- To develop large muscles

LEARNING OBJECTIVE:
Using a camel riding stick, the children will race.

MATERIALS:
Camel head pattern (Appendix A28)
Pencil
Poster board
Crayons, markers, or colored pencils
Scissors
Empty gift wrap tubes
Stapler and staples
Newspaper
Masking tape
Chalk
Globe
Optional: Whistle and handkerchief

DISCUSSION SUGGESTIONS:
- In Qatar, boys are trained as camel jockeys. They race for 5–7 miles.
- The boys wear pants with Velcro bottoms that hold them in the Velcro-patched saddle (Augustin & Augustin, 1997).

ADULT PREPARATION:
1. Trace the camel head pattern on poster board.
2. Cut out and color one camel head for each child.
3. Insert the neck of the camel head into the empty gift wrap tube.
4. Staple the head into place.
5. Roll newspaper into a tight cylinder.
6. Insert the newspaper into the empty gift wrap tube to strengthen it.
7. Tape the end of the wrapping paper tube to hold the newspaper in place.

continued

Qatar's Camel Racing continued

8. Repeat steps 1–7 making a camel riding stick for each child.

9. Mark a start and a finish line outdoors with masking tape or chalk.

PROCEDURES:

The children will complete the following steps:

1. Find the state he or she lives in on the globe with the adult's assistance.

2. Find Qatar on the globe with the adult's assistance. Note the distance between the two.

3. Listen to the adult explain that camel racing is a sport in Qatar.

4. Select a camel riding stick and mount their camel.

5. Line up at the starting line with their camel.

6. Watch the adult for the starting signal, which may be a whistle, the drop of a handkerchief, or simply saying, "GO!"

NOTES:

✄ Children may color their own camel head.

✄ Adults may make fewer camel riding sticks and require children to take turns racing.

Queens and Kings

DISCUSSION SUGGESTIONS:

- ✄ In some countries, such as England, Norway, and Denmark, they still have people who are called queens or kings.
- ✄ England has Queen Elizabeth II, Norway has King Harald V, and Denmark has Queen Margrethe II.
- ✄ Most days, the queens and kings dress like ordinary people. On very special occasions, they might dress in ceremonial costumes, and they might be allowed to wear their crown. The crowns are very valuable and are usually kept in locked places for safety.
- ✄ Some people curtsy or bow to queens and kings as a sign of respect and honor.

ADULT PREPARATION:

1. Cut construction paper into 5" strips.
2. Staple strips together to make hat bands for each child. Write children's names on their hat band.
3. Put plastic gems in a bowl.

PROCEDURES:

The child will complete the following steps:

1. Listen to the adult read a book about kings and queens.
2. Select the hat band with his or her name written on it.
3. Create a crown by gluing plastic gems on the hat band.
4. Allow the glue to dry.
5. Practice bowing or curtsying while wearing the crown.

BOOK SUGGESTION:

May I Bring A Friend? by Beatrice Schenk de Regniers (New York: Atheneum, 1964). A boy is invited to the king and queen's house.

AGES: 3–5

GROUP SIZE:
3–10 children

DEVELOPMENTAL GOALS:

- ✄ To acquire an awareness for the culture of people around the world
- ✄ To develop creativity

LEARNING OBJECTIVE:
Using hat bands, glue, plastic gems, and a book, the child will practice curtsying or bowing to show respect.

MATERIALS:
Construction paper
Scissors
Ruler
Stapler and staples
Marker
Plastic gems
Bowl
Glue
Book about queens and kings

Q

Quoits Game

AGES: 3–5

GROUP SIZE:
2–4 children

DEVELOPMENTAL GOALS:
- ✂ To develop a sense of history
- ✂ To coordinate large muscle development

LEARNING OBJECTIVE:
Using wooden or plastic rings and stakes, the children will play a game played centuries ago.

MATERIALS:
Four 12"–18" wooden or plastic stakes
Hammer
3' length of rope
Plastic rings approximately 12"–15" in diameter

DISCUSSION SUGGESTIONS:

1. The game of *quoits* was played 2,000 years ago in Greece. It was played in the Olympic Games.
2. English settlers brought *quoits* to America in the 1700s.
3. *Quoits* was first played with iron rings. In colonial America, they found horseshoes worked just as well.
4. By the 1800s, horseshoes replaced *quoits* in popularity.
5. To play *quoits,* the rings are tossed at a stake in the ground. Each player throws two rings. If a ring circles the stake, it's worth two points. If no one's ring is around the stake, the one closest to the stake gets one point. The first one to 21 points wins.
6. Colonial children either played with two or four players. If there were four players, they divided into two teams.
7. The wealthy colonial children played with iron rings. Others made their own rings out of leather, rope, or willow branches (King, 1998).

ADULT PREPARATION:

1. Hammer stake into the ground.
2. Depending upon the children's abilities to toss a ring, lay the length of rope down on the ground 6'–20' from the stake.
3. Decide if the children will play for points, and if so, how high will the points go?

continued

Quoits Game continued

PROCEDURES:

The children will complete the following steps:

1. Take turns lining up behind the rope.

2. Throw a ring at the stake, attempting to circle the stake.

3. Repeat step 2 with a second ring.

4. Leave the two rings in place and allow the next player to throw the additional two rings.

5. If points are being kept, check to see if any rings circle the stake. If they did, it is worth two points. If no one's ring is around the stake, check to see whose ring is closest. That ring is worth one point.

NOTES:

✂ Most preschoolers' attention spans will not last for 21 points. Set a lower number before playing, or play without points.

✂ Younger children should not play for points, but only play for the joy of doing it.

✂ If plastic rings are not available, rings can be created by taping a 12"–15" length of rope into circles.

R

Ranger

AGES: 3–5

GROUP SIZE:
2–10 children

DEVELOPMENTAL GOALS:
- ✂ To explore different occupations
- ✂ To promote social development

LEARNING OBJECTIVE:
Using stuffed animals, a brown shirt, brown hat, and a ranger badge, the children will take turns leading others on a hike.

MATERIALS:
Ranger badge (Appendix A29)
Yellow copy paper
Scissors
Permanent marker
Hole punch
Ruler
String
Stuffed animals
Brown hat
Brown shirt

DISCUSSION SUGGESTIONS:

- ✂ Rangers work in parks. Most of the time they work outdoors.
- ✂ They may help lead hikes and tours of the park.
- ✂ Rangers make sure people are safe at the campgrounds and that people are practicing fire safety if they make campfires.
- ✂ They have to be available to answer questions from visitors.
- ✂ Some rangers help teach classes about different things in the park such as plants, animals, and geography.
- ✂ Rangers have to know first aid, so they can help people if they are injured.

ADULT PREPARATION:

1. Copy and cut out a ranger badge for each child from the yellow copy paper.
2. Write each child's name on the back of his or her badge.

continued

Ranger continued

3. Punch a hole in the badge and thread a 12" string through the hole. Knot the ends together.

4. Hide stuffed animals outside.

PROCEDURES:

The children will complete the following steps:

1. Assign a child to be the ranger.

2. Put on the badge, with his or her name, like a necklace.

3. Put on the brown hat and shirt.

4. Lead others around the playground; point out animals, plants, or trees that are found.

5. Allow other children to take a turn being the ranger and repeat steps 2–4.

Repair Person

AGES: 4–5

GROUP SIZE:
2–4 children

DEVELOPMENTAL GOALS:

✂ To appreciate different occupations

✂ To enhance fine motor skills

LEARNING OBJECTIVE:
Using tools and small appliances, the children will take things apart and attempt to put them back together.

MATERIALS:
Heavy-duty scissors or wire cutters
Small broken appliances
Flathead screwdrivers
Phillips screwdrivers
Book about a repair person
Small bowls

DISCUSSION SUGGESTIONS:

✂ A repair person fixes things that are broken.

✂ They use tools like screwdrivers, pliers, and hammers.

✂ A repair person knows how to take things apart and fix them, then put them back together.

✂ A repair person fixes things like television sets, computers, washing machines, dryers, and radios.

✂ Some repair persons only fix one type of equipment, like a television repair person or computer repair person.

ADULT PREPARATION:

1. Cut the cords off small broken appliances.

2. Look for any hazards in the appliances such as sharp objects.

3. Set out screwdrivers, both flathead and Phillips types.

continued

Repair Person continued

PROCEDURES:

The children will complete the following steps:

1. Listen to a story about a repair person.

2. Take turns using screwdrivers to take appliances apart and put them back together.

3. When removing screws, put the screws in a small bowl to prevent them from getting lost.

SAFETY PRECAUTION:

Supervise children closely when using small objects, such as screws, to prevent choking hazards.

BOOK SUGGESTION:

Fix-It by David McPhail (New York: E.P. Dutton, 1984). Emma wants to watch television but it's not working. Father calls the repair man.

R

GROUP SIZE:
2–3 children

DEVELOPMENTAL GOALS:
- ✂ To appreciate another culture's art form
- ✂ To sequence objects by size

LEARNING OBJECTIVE:
Using varying sizes of nesting doll cutouts, the child will sequence them by size.

MATERIALS:
Russian nesting doll patterns (Appendix A30)
Copy paper
Scissors
Colored pencils
Globe
Nesting cups

Russian Nesting Dolls

DISCUSSION SUGGESTIONS:
- ✂ Russian nesting dolls are a set of toys made out of wood.
- ✂ The dolls are meant to be a family.
- ✂ The dolls fit inside one another. The smallest one is one piece. The sequentially larger ones open up into two pieces, so the smaller ones fit inside. The largest doll holds them all.
- ✂ In Russia, they are called *matryoshka* (Murrell, 1998).

ADULT PREPARATION:
1. Copy and cut out various sizes of the Russian doll nesting pattern. Cut a minimum of 3 for two-year-olds, and up to 12 for five-year-olds.
2. Color the nesting doll cutouts with colored pencils.

PROCEDURES:
The child will complete the following steps:
1. Find the state he or she lives in on the globe with the adult's assistance.
2. Find Russia on the globe with the adult's assistance. Note the distance between the two.
3. Listen to adult explain that colorful wooden dolls are made in Russia, where the dolls can be taken apart and then fit inside each other. They fit inside each other like nesting cups.
4. Use nesting cups to stack one inside the other.
5. Set nesting cups aside to use the nesting doll cutouts.
6. Find the largest nesting doll cutout and place it on the left.
7. Find the doll slightly smaller and place it to the right of the first cutout.
8. Continue to sequence the nesting doll cutouts until all have been found, placing them from largest to smallest.

VARIATION:
If actual nesting dolls are available, use them in place of the cutouts.

EXPANSION:
Have the child put together nesting cups, or nesting measuring cups.

Sharing

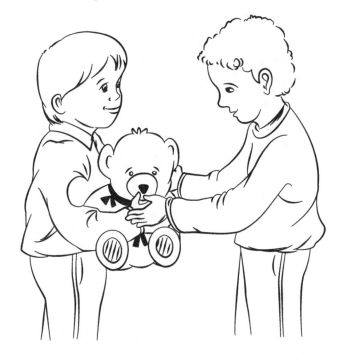

AGES: 3–5

GROUP SIZE:
4–20 children

DEVELOPMENTAL GOALS:
- ✂ To develop prosocial behaviors
- ✂ To treat others with respect

LEARNING OBJECTIVE:
Using a song board, the children will sing a song about sharing.

MATERIALS:
Poster board
Markers
Masking tape

DISCUSSION SUGGESTIONS:
- ✂ It is necessary to share.
- ✂ People share rooms, toys, books, and many other things.
- ✂ "What types of things do you share?"

ADULT PREPARATION:
1. Using a poster board and markers, write the words to the sharing song written below.
2. Hang the poster in the group time area at the children's eye level using masking tape.

PROCEDURES:
The children will complete the following steps:
1. Stand in a circle in the group time area.
2. Hold hands, walking around in the circle as they sing the following song to the tune of *It's Raining, It's Pouring, the Old Man is Snoring.*

continued

Sharing continued

Sharing

We're sharing, we're sharing,
We're sharing because we're caring,
We share our toys, without a fuss,
We share because we care, we care.

S

Spanish Gazpacho

DISCUSSION SUGGESTIONS:

- Spanish *gazpacho* is a chilled soup with uncooked vegetables.
- It originated as a way to use up overripe vegetables.
- It was thought to be peasant fare (Jordan, 1996).

ADULT PREPARATION:

1. Wash hands.
2. Wash vegetables and set aside.
3. Peel cucumber and place on a cutting board to cut into small pieces.
4. Place cucumber pieces in a bowl.
5. Chop Roma tomatoes into small pieces and place them in a bowl.
6. Cut ½ of green pepper into small pieces and place them in a bowl.
7. Chop ½ of small red onion into small pieces and place them in a bowl.
8. Use a can puncher and make two triangular holes in the top of the vegetable juice can.
9. Measure 1 teaspoon lemon juice and place in a small bowl.

PROCEDURES:

The children will complete the following steps:

1. Find the state he or she lives in on the globe with the adult's assistance.
2. Find Spain on the globe with the adult's assistance. Note the distance between the two.
3. Listen to adult explain that *gazpacho* is a cold soup made in Spain.
4. Wash hands.
5. Take turns adding the following ingredients into the plastic container:
   a. Green pepper
   b. Red onion
   c. Cucumber
   d. Vegetable juice
   e. Lemon juice
   f. Dash of salt
   g. Dash of pepper

continued

AGES: 3–5

GROUP SIZE:

6–8 children

DEVELOPMENTAL GOALS:

- To appreciate another culture's food
- To practice cooking procedures

LEARNING OBJECTIVE:

Using Roma tomatoes, cucumber, green bell pepper, vegetable juice, salt, pepper, large plastic container with lid, and a spoon, the children will work together to make gazpacho.

MATERIALS:

Small cucumber
3 Roma tomatoes
Small green bell pepper
Small red onion
Vegetable peeler
Cutting board
Knife
Bowls
Can puncher
46 ounce can of vegetable juice

MATERIALS:

Measuring spoons
Lemon juice
Small bowl
Globe
Large plastic container
   with lid
Salt
Pepper
Long-handled spoon

Spanish Gazpacho continued

6. Stir well with a long-handled spoon.

The adult will complete the following steps:

1. Put the lid on the plastic container.

2. Refrigerate for 24 hours.

3. Serve at snack or lunch time.

⚠ SAFETY PRECAUTIONS:

✂ Supervise children closely when eating small items such as the cut vegetables, to prevent choking.

✂ Check for food allergies in children before doing any cooking activity.

NOTE:

Older children may help cut the vegetables.

Sweden's St. Lucia Day

AGES: 3–5

GROUP SIZE:
2–5 children

DEVELOPMENTAL GOALS:

- ✄ To develop a sense of appreciation for the ways of others
- ✄ To stimulate small muscle development

LEARNING OBJECTIVE:

Using a white paper plate, green tissue paper, glue, and construction paper flames, the child will create a St. Lucia crown.

MATERIALS:

Copy paper
St. Lucia crown pattern (Appendix A31)
Pencil
White paper plates
Scissors
Flame pattern (Appendix A11)
Yellow construction paper

DISCUSSION SUGGESTIONS:

- ✄ St. Lucia Day is the Swedish "festival of lights" celebrated on December 13th.
- ✄ The girls dress as St. Lucia and wear white dresses and a crown of greenery with candles. These may be real or battery-operated candles.
- ✄ The boys wear pointed cone-shaped hats with a golden star. They are called Star Boys.
- ✄ In Sweden, the oldest daughter will dress as St. Lucia and serve their family a breakfast of coffee and pastries in bed.
- ✄ Throughout the day, the children dress as St. Lucia and Star Boys.

continued

Sweden's St. Lucia Day continued

MATERIALS:

Green tissue paper
Ruler
Marker
Globe
Glue

ADULT PREPARATION:

1. Make a copy of the St. Lucia crown pattern.
2. Trace and cut the St. Lucia crown pattern out of a white paper plate—one for each child.
3. Fold the candles of the crown upright.
4. Trace and cut the flame pattern out of yellow construction paper.
5. Cut tissue paper into 6" squares, to enable children to handle it more easily.
6. Write each child's name on an individual paper plate crown.

PROCEDURES:

The child will complete the following steps:

1. Find the state he or she lives in on the globe with the adult's assistance.
2. Find Sweden on the globe with the adult's assistance. Note the distance between the two.
3. Select the paper plate crown with his or her name.
4. Tear and glue pieces of green tissue paper to the brim of the crown, creating a wreath.
5. Glue a flame to the top of each candle.

EXPANSION:

Once the St. Lucia crown is dry, the children may use it in dramatic play to act out the eldest daughter serving the family in bed.

Telling the Truth

DISCUSSION SUGGESTIONS:

- ✂ We should always tell the truth.
- ✂ The truth is what really happens.
- ✂ A lie is the opposite of the truth. A lie is when we do not tell everything that we know happened.
- ✂ Telling the truth is very important.

ADULT PREPARATION:

1. Create a song board by writing the words to *Telling the Truth* on a poster board.

PROCEDURES:

The children will complete the following steps:

1. Listen to a book read about telling the truth.
2. The children will sing the words to the following song to the tune of *Mary Had a Little Lamb.*

Telling the Truth

Telling the truth is easy to do.

Easy to do,

Easy to do.

Telling the truth is easy to do.

Just state the facts as they are true.

No need to remember what was said,

What was said,

What was said,

No need to remember what was said.

By telling the truth you have nothing to dread.

BOOK SUGGESTIONS:

- ✂ *Franklin Fibs* by Paulette Bourgeois (New York: Scholastic, Inc. 1991). Franklin tells a lie and then finds out the consequence of his fib as he tries to keep his friends from uncovering the truth.
- ✂ *I Am Honest* by Angela Leeper (Chicago: Heinemann Library, 2005). Honesty is explored with simple sentences and color photographs.

T

AGES: 3–5

GROUP SIZE:

6–12 children

DEVELOPMENTAL GOALS:

- ✂ To understand the need for telling the truth
- ✂ To develop successful social interactions

LEARNING OBJECTIVE:

Using a song board, the children will sing a song about the importance of telling the truth.

MATERIALS:

Poster board
Markers
Book about telling the truth

Timeline

AGES: 3–5

GROUP SIZE:
2–4 children

DEVELOPMENTAL GOALS:
- ✂ To build knowledge
- ✂ To examine collective information

LEARNING OBJECTIVE:
Using birthday cake cutouts and art materials, the children will assist in making a timeline.

MATERIALS:
Birthday cake pattern (Appendix A32)
Copy paper
Tagboard or poster board
Pencil
Scissors
Tempera paint
Paint containers
Tablespoon
Dish soap
Paintbrushes
Smock
Permanent marker
Construction paper
Masking tape

DISCUSSION SUGGESTIONS:
- ✂ Timelines are a certain length of time.
- ✂ Timelines focus on events that go in sequential order (i.e., what happened first, what happened next?").
- ✂ A timeline could consist of many different things (e.g., the dates different dolls were created, or the dates a child sat up, crawled, and walked, could be placed on a timeline).

ADULT PREPARATION:
1. Copy and cut out one birthday cake for each child from tagboard or poster board.
2. Pour tempera paint into paint containers. Use a separate container for each color.
3. Add 1 tablespoon of dish soap to the paint; stir with the spoon.
4. Place a paintbrush with the paint. Use one brush for each color of paint.

PROCEDURES:
The children will complete the following steps:
1. Put on a smock.
2. Using a paintbrush, paint the birthday cake cutout with paint.

The adult will complete the following steps:
1. When the birthday cake cutouts are dry, write the child's name and birth date on the cake with a permanent marker.
2. Write the names of the months on separate sheets of construction paper.
3. Tape each month in sequential order on the wall with masking tape.
4. Tape each painted birthday cake under the correct month in numerical order.
5. Explain to the children:
   a. A timeline is a certain length of time.
   b. Their timeline is a year of birthdays.

NOTE:
Children may help sequence the order of the cakes and put them on the wall.

Truck Driver

T

AGES: 3–5

GROUP SIZE:
2–5 children

DEVELOPMENTAL
GOALS:
⚹ To value different
occupations
⚹ To develop
imagination
through role-
playing

LEARNING
OBJECTIVE:
Using chairs, boxes,
and toys, the children
will pretend to be truck
drivers.

MATERIALS:
Two sizes of boxes
Chairs
Plastic plate
Stuffed animals
Plastic food
Toys
Book about trucks
Map

DISCUSSION SUGGESTIONS:

⚹ Some people drive a truck for their job.

⚹ Some drive big trucks, called a semi, that have a bed where they can sleep.

⚹ Some drive smaller trucks and work close to home.

⚹ Truck drivers deliver many things, such as furniture, food, animals, milk, or gasoline.

⚹ A truck driver may have a refrigerated truck to keep food cold.

⚹ To drive a big truck, a person needs a special driver's license.

ADULT PREPARATION:

1. Place two chairs side by side. Place a plate on one chair for the steering wheel.

2. Place a box behind the chairs to "load" items for delivery.

3. Place food, stuffed animals, toys, etc. on a table.

continued

Truck Driver continued

PROCEDURES:

The children will complete the following steps:

1. Listen to a book about trucks.
2. Assign roles of truck driver and helper.
3. Select items to "load on the truck" (put in the box).
4. Load the items into the truck's bed (box).
5. Look at the map to check directions.
6. Sit in the chairs.
7. Use the plastic plate as a steering wheel to "drive" to a location.
8. Remove the items from the truck's bed (box).
9. Sit in the chairs and "drive" back to the first location.
10. Repeat steps 1–8 with other children.

BOOK SUGGESTION:

Trucks by Darlene Stille (New York: Children's Press, 1997). Various trucks are discussed in this book.

EXPANSION:

Use assorted trucks and small toys on a road mat or in the block area.

Ugandan Drinks

DISCUSSION SUGGESTIONS:

- ✁ Coffee is the largest crop in Uganda.
- ✁ Coffee grows from a tree. The beverage is made from the seeds of its fruit, or berries.
- ✁ Tea is the third-largest crop in Uganda.
- ✁ Tea is made from the dried leaves of a plant.

ADULT PREPARATION:

1. Put coffee grounds and loose-leaf tea in separate large bowls.

PROCEDURES:

The child will complete the following steps:

1. Find the state he or she lives in on the globe with the adult's assistance.
2. Find Uganda on the globe with the adult's assistance. Note the distance between the two.
3. Listen to adult explain that coffee and tea are grown in Uganda.
4. Examine coffee grounds and tea leaves by using a magnifying glass.
5. Examine the coffee grounds and tea leaves by sifting them through fingers.
6. State the difference between the coffee grounds and the tea leaves.

EXPANSIONS:

- ✁ Check center's policies. If permissible, brew coffee and tea to allow children do to a taste test. Do not serve the children hot beverages. The liquids should only be warm. Parent permission may be obtained and decaffeinated beverages may be used, as some groups forbid the use of caffeine for both children and adults.
- ✁ Brew extra-strength coffee and tea. Allow the children to tie-dye prewashed white cloth pieces using the coffee and tea as dyes.

AGES: 3–5

GROUP SIZE:
2–4 children

DEVELOPMENTAL GOALS:
- ✁ To develop global connections
- ✁ To distinguish similarities and differences

LEARNING OBJECTIVE:
Using coffee grounds, loose-leaf tea, and a magnifying glass, the child will observe similarities and differences.

MATERIALS:
Coffee grounds
Loose-leaf tea
Large bowls
Globe
Magnifying glass

Uniforms

AGES: 3–5

GROUP SIZE:

2–4 children

DEVELOPMENTAL GOALS:

✂ To identify community helpers

✂ To develop classification skills

LEARNING OBJECTIVE:

Using picture cards of uniforms and people at work, the child will match the uniform to the occupation.

MATERIALS:

Uniform patterns (Appendix A33–A36)
Police officer (Appendix A33)
Mail carrier (Appendix A34)
Doctor (Appendix A35)
Dental hygienist (Appendix A36)
Pictures of people at work in their uniforms (Appendix A37–A40)
Police officer at police station (Appendix A37)

DISCUSSION SUGGESTIONS:

✂ A uniform is a type of clothing that is the same for everyone in that particular place.

✂ Sport teams have uniforms. Some schools have uniforms. Some jobs have uniforms.

✂ Uniforms make a statement that a person belongs to a specific group.

✂ Who have you seen wear a uniform?

ADULT PREPARATION:

1. Copy and cut out uniform patterns and pictures of people at work in their uniforms.

2. If desired, color the uniforms and the pictures. Make sure to color the uniform the same in the matching picture for younger children.

3. Cut construction paper into squares.

4. Glue the uniforms and pictures on individual squares of construction paper using the rubber cement.

5. Lay the pictures of people at work on the table face up.

6. Lay the pictures of uniforms on the table face down.

PROCEDURES:

The child will complete the following steps:

1. Listen to a book about people wearing occupational uniforms.

2. Look at the pictures of people at work.

3. Identify the occupations in the pictures.

4. Turn over one uniform picture.

5. Identify the uniform (e.g., doctor's white coat).

6. Place the uniform picture with the matching picture of the person at work.

7. Repeat steps 2–6 until all uniforms have been matched with the correct occupation.

NOTE:

Additional uniform cards may be made by using uniform catalogues or pictures from the Internet.

continued

Uniforms continued

BOOK SUGGESTION:

Read *Whose Shoes are These?* By Laura Purdie Salas (Minneapolis, MN: Picture Window Books, 2006). This book matches shoes with occupations.

MATERIALS:

Mail carrier delivering mail (Appendix A38)
Doctor in the office with a patient (Appendix A39)
Dental hygienist cleaning teeth (Appendix A40)
Copy paper
Scissors
Construction paper
Markers, colored pencils, or crayons
Rubber cement
Book about people wearing occupational uniforms

AGES: 3–5

GROUP SIZE:
6–16 children

DEVELOPMENTAL GOALS:

- ✂ To develop the concept of geography
- ✂ To recognize family members

LEARNING OBJECTIVE:

Using a map and a list of family members, the children will plot where relatives live.

MATERIALS:

Copy paper
Family Letter 5 (Appendix B6)
Poster board
Large map of the United States
Rubber cement or masking tape
Small stickers
Book about extended families who live far away

United States and Families

DISCUSSION SUGGESTIONS:

- ✂ Some families all live together in the same house or in the same town.
- ✂ Many families are not able to live close to each other.
- ✂ People have to live close to their jobs or schools.
- ✂ Some people grow up and then have to move far from their families.
- ✂ Grandchildren may not live near their grandparents. Cousins may live far apart. Nieces and aunts or nephews and uncles may live in different parts of the country.
- ✂ When families live far apart, they do not get to see each other very often.

ADULT PREPARATION:

1. Copy the family letter and send it home with the children.
2. Place a map on a poster board with rubber cement or masking tape.

continued

United States and Families continued

PROCEDURES:

The children will complete the following steps:

1. Sit in a circle or semicircle for group time.
2. Identify family members and the state they live in with the adult's assistance.
3. Place a sticker on the state where the family member lives.
4. Once all the children have plotted where their relatives live, count the number of stickers in each state.

NOTE:

Depending on the size of the map, small pictures of family members may be used instead of stickers.

BOOK SUGGESTION:

The Relatives Came by Cynthia Rylant (New York: Bradbury Press, 1985). The relatives come to visit from Virginia.

EXPANSION:

Make a class graph of the states which have at least one relative.

AGES: 3–5

GROUP SIZE:
2–3 children

DEVELOPMENTAL GOALS:

✂ To experience another culture

✂ To participate in a group project

LEARNING OBJECTIVE:

Using ingredients and cooking equipment, the children will work together to make Venezuelan *arepas*.

MATERIALS:

Baking sheet
Aluminum foil
Corn flour
Shredded white cheese such as mozzarella
Salt
Water
Bowls
Mixing bowl
Measuring spoons
Measuring cups
Whisk
Nonstick electric skillet or griddle
Masking tape
Towels

Venezuelan Bread: Arepas

DISCUSSION SUGGESTIONS:

✂ *Arepas* in Venezuela are like bread in other countries.

✂ *Arepas* are commonly made in Venezuela and served as a side item for a meal or may be eaten alone.

✂ Small restaurants that serve only *arepas* are called *areperas*. They may serve the *arepas* with cheese, jam, eggs, or meat (Risso, 2001).

ADULT PREPARATION:

1. Wash hands.
2. Cover the baking sheet with aluminum foil.
3. Put corn flour, salt, shredded white cheese, and water in separate bowls.
4. Preheat the oven to 350°.
5. Set the electric skillet on the table. Plug it into an outlet. Tape the electric cord to the table and floor, so no one will accidentally pull the appliance by the cord.
6. Roll towels and place them around the skillet to prevent burning.

PROCEDURES:

The children will complete the following steps:

1. Find the state he or she lives in on the globe with the adult's assistance.
2. Find Venezuela on the globe with the adult's assistance. Note the distance between the two.
3. Wash hands.
4. Each child may add following ingredients in the mixing bowl:

   a. ¼ cup corn flour

   b. One pinch of salt

   c. 1 tablespoon of grated white cheese

continued

120

Venezuelan Bread: Arepas continued

5. Use the whisk to mix the ingredients together.

6. Slowly add ¼ cup of water while stirring, making a firm but moist dough.

7. Form the dough into a ball and then set it on a plate to flatten it.

The adult will complete the following steps:

1. Set the electric skillet or griddle on medium.

2. Add 2 tablespoons of olive oil to grease the skillet.

3. Cook the *arepas* on each side until golden brown.

4. Place each child's *arepas* on the foil covered baking sheet. Write the child's name under the *arepas* with a permanent marker.

5. Bake in the oven for 20–25 minutes, turning them at least one time.

6. Drain and rinse black beans in a colander and place them in a bowl.

7. Write children's names on the edge of individual paper plates with a permanent marker.

8. Place each child's *arepas* on their labeled plate.

The children will complete the following steps:

1. Wash hands.

2. Select the plate with his or her name.

3. Place a spoonful of black beans on the plate.

4. Eat for lunch or snack.

SAFETY PRECAUTIONS:

✄ Supervise children constantly when using a hot appliance. Check with your center's policies regarding cooking in the classroom. If cooking is not allowed in the classroom, use the electric skillet or griddle in the kitchen.

✄ Check for food allergies before beginning any cooking procedure.

MATERIALS:

Globe
Permanent marker
15 oz. can of black beans
Colander
Bowl
Spoon
Paper plates

Veterinarian

GROUP SIZE:

2–4 children

DEVELOPMENTAL GOALS:

✂ To gain knowledge of different occupations

✂ To practice role-playing

LEARNING OBJECTIVE:

Using stuffed animals, toy stethoscope, toy syringe, and chairs, the children will role-play veterinarian and pet owner.

MATERIALS:

Marker
Construction paper
Masking tape
Book about a
   veterinarian
Stuffed animals
Optional: pet carrier,
   leashes, collars, and
   dog biscuits
Chairs
Table
Toy stethoscope
Toy syringe

DISCUSSION SUGGESTIONS:

✂ Veterinarians are often called a "vet."

✂ They are a doctor for animals.

✂ They go to school to learn how to take care of the animals and to learn to do different types of surgery that animals need.

✂ Vets give the animals immunizations, or shots.

✂ They give the animals checkups to make sure they are healthy.

ADULT PREPARATION:

1. Write veterinarian on a piece of construction paper; tape it to the wall or table.

2. Set chairs in a row for customers to sit and wait.

continued

122

Veterinarian continued

PROCEDURES:

The children will complete the following steps:

1. Listen to a book about a veterinarian
2. Answer the adult's question, "What does a veterinarian do?"
3. Notice veterinarian sign on the wall.
4. Assign roles of veterinarian and pet owner(s).
5. The pet owner(s) will:
    a. Select a stuffed animal for their pet.
    b. Optional: Put a collar and leash on the animal or put them in a pet carrier.
    c. Sit in a chair and wait for the veterinarian to call their name.
6. The veterinarian will call a pet owner's name and ask the name of his or her pet.
7. The pet owner will place his or her pet on the table.
8. The veterinarian will:
    a. Look at the pet's ears and eyes.
    b. Listen to the pet's heartbeat with the toy stethoscope.
    c. Give the pet his or her vaccinations with the toy syringe.
    d. Optional: Give the pet a biscuit for behaving well.
9. Switch roles and repeat steps 4–8.

NOTE:

Adult may need to use rubbing alcohol and cotton balls to clean the stethoscope between each child's use of the instrument.

BOOK SUGGESTION:

Come to the Doctor, Harry by Mary Chalmers (New York: Harper Collins Children's Books, 1981). A cat hurts his tail and is afraid to go to the vet.

Voting

AGES: 3½–5

GROUP SIZE:

2–4 children

DEVELOPMENTAL GOALS:

✂ To develop an awareness of belonging to a group

✂ To develop skills for successful citizen participation

LEARNING OBJECTIVE:

Using children's books, baskets, and counters, the children will participate in the voting process.

MATERIALS:

Two children's books
Three baskets
Chips or counters
A book about voting

DISCUSSION SUGGESTIONS:

✂ Voting is when a group of people get to make a choice between at least two things.

✂ The choice that the largest numbers of people want is considered the winner.

✂ Voting is done in countries where people have a choice who will be the leaders.

✂ In the United States, a person has to be at least 18-years-old to vote in government elections.

✂ Anyone can vote with an informal group. People can vote for their favorite ice cream, a song to be sung, or a favorite book.

continued

Voting continued

ADULT PREPARATION:

1. Set two books on a table.
2. Place a basket in front of each book.
3. Place chips or counters in a third basket.

PROCEDURES:

The children will complete the following steps:

1. Listen to a book about voting.
2. Take a chip out of the basket.
3. Look at the two books on the table.
4. Vote for the book they would like read to the group by placing their chip in the basket in front of the book.
5. Count the number of chips in each basket.
6. Decide which number is higher and which book won.
7. Listen to the winning book.

NOTE:

This is an introductory voting activity. Children may vote on many things, such as what to eat for snack, visitors to have in the classroom, etc.

BOOK SUGGESTION:

Vote! By Eileen Christelow (New York: Clarion Books, 2003). The voting process is discussed in two formats. Each page contains factual information and cartoons with characters speaking about a fictional election.

Wales' Sheep

AGES: 3–5

GROUP SIZE:

2–3 children

DEVELOPMENTAL GOALS:

✂ To develop a sense of geography

✂ To enhance number recognition

LEARNING OBJECTIVE:

Using sheep cutouts and wool yarn pieces, the child will identify numbers and practice rational counting.

MATERIALS:

Copy paper
Sheep pattern
    (Appendix A41)
Pencil
Construction paper
Scissors
Permanent marker
Ruler
Wool yarn
Bowl
Globe
Tweezers or spring
    clothespins

DISCUSSION SUGGESTIONS:

✂ In Wales, there are twice as many sheep as people.

✂ They are raised for wool and meat (Hestler, 2001).

ADULT PREPARATION:

1. Make a copy of the sheep pattern.

2. Trace and cut out 11 sheep out of construction paper.

3. Write the numbers 0–10 on the sheep cutouts with a permanent marker.

4. Cut the yarn into fifty-five 2" lengths.

5. Place the yarn pieces in a bowl.

PROCEDURES:

The child will complete the following steps:

1. Find the state he or she lives in on the globe with the adult's assistance.

2. Find Wales on the globe with the adult's assistance. Note the distance between the two.

3. Listen to adult explain that they raise sheep in Wales, and people get wool from sheep.

4. Identify the number on the sheep.

5. Use the tweezers and place that specific number of wool yarn pieces on the sheep.

6. Repeat steps 4–5 until all sheep (except 0) have wool yarn on them.

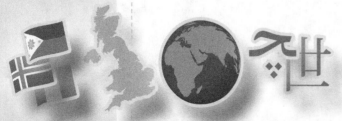

Weather Forecaster

DISCUSSION SUGGESTIONS:

✂ Most weather forecasters also have to be a meteorologist.

✂ To be a meteorologist requires at least four years of college.

✂ Weather forecasters have to be trained to read science equipment to help predict the weather (People at Work, 2005).

ADULT PREPARATION:

1. Copy and cut out umbrellas on blue construction paper.
2. Copy and cut out suns on yellow construction paper.
3. Copy and cut out clouds on gray construction paper.
4. Copy and cut out snowflakes on white construction paper.
5. Hang the state map and the United States map at the children's eye level.
6. Cut hook and loop tape into sections.
7. Place one side of the hook and loop tape on the map. Place the other sections on the back of the weather symbols.
8. Put the weather symbols in a basket.

PROCEDURES:

The child will complete the following steps:

1. Use the pointer to emphasize certain areas of the maps.
2. Say what the weather is doing in that area and place the corresponding weather symbol on the map.

BOOK SUGGESTION:

Weather ABC by B. A. Hoena (Mankato, MN: Capstone Press, 2005). Weather vocabulary is introduced with photographs in an ABC format.

NOTE:

To preserve the weather symbols and maps when using hook and loop tape, it is recommended that the maps and symbols are laminated or covered with clear contact paper.

continued

AGES: 3–5

GROUP SIZE:
2–3 children

DEVELOPMENTAL GOALS:

✂ To role-play an occupation

✂ To demonstrate knowledge of the weather

LEARNING OBJECTIVE:

Using the state map, the United States map, a pointer, and weather symbols, the child will act out the role of weather forecaster.

MATERIALS:

Blue, yellow, gray, and white card stock paper
Weather symbols patterns (Appendix A42–A45)
Umbrella (Appendix A42)
Sun (Appendix A43)
Cloud (Appendix A44)
Snowflake (Appendix A45)

Weather Forecaster continued

MATERIALS:

Scissors
State map
United States map
Masking tape
Hook and loop tape
Pointer
Basket

EXPANSIONS:

✂ Many city newspapers have a United States map showing the weather forecast, with symbols for different areas. Show the children this weather map and allow them to duplicate it by placing the appropriate symbols on the hanging map.

✂ Create a weather wheel by dividing a white paper plate into quarters with a permanent marker. Children may glue one of the four weather symbols in each quarter. Give each child a spring clothespin and allow them to check the weather daily and fix their clothespin to the symbol representing the current weather.

128

X-Ray Technician

AGES: 3–5

GROUP SIZE:
2 children

DEVELOPMENTAL GOALS:

- ✂ To explore various occupations
- ✂ To stimulate social development

LEARNING OBJECTIVE:

Using a cot, cardboard with a plus sign centered on it, plastic smocks, and a standing divider, the children will role-play X-ray technician and patient.

MATERIALS:

Marker
Ruler
Cardboard (12″ × 18″)
Cot
Standing divider
Book about X-rays
Plastic smocks

DISCUSSION SUGGESTIONS:

- ✂ An X-ray technician is the person whose job requires them to take X-rays of people.
- ✂ An X-ray is a special type of photograph made with radiation.
- ✂ An X-ray technician has to go to school to learn how to use the machine and how to look at an X-ray.
- ✂ An X-ray technician knows where to place the machine to get the picture the doctor needs.
- ✂ An X-ray technician may wear a uniform like a nurse or a doctor.
- ✂ He or she may work in a hospital or in a doctor's office.

ADULT PREPARATION:

1. Use the marker to make a 9″ plus symbol (+) in the center of the cardboard.
2. Lay the cardboard on the cot with the "+" facing up.
3. Set the standing divider 2–3 feet from the cot.

continued

X-Ray Technician continued

PROCEDURES:

The children will complete the following steps:

1. Listen to a book about X-rays.

2. Assign roles of patient and X-ray technician.

3. Both the patient and the X-ray technician will put on smocks.

4. The technician will direct the patient to sit on the cot, and will position his or her leg over the center of the cardboard.

5. The technician will stand behind the divider and instruct the patient to lie very still.

6. The technician will make a buzzing noise to indicate the X-ray is being taken.

7. Once the buzzing stops, the technician will return to the patient and instruct them to lay their arm on the center of the cardboard.

8. Repeat steps 3–6, X-raying other body parts.

9. When the X-ray technician has finished taking X-rays, the technician and patient may switch roles and repeat steps 3–7.

BOOK SUGGESTION:

Jessica's X-Ray by Pat Zonta (Toronto, Ontario: Firefly Books, 2002). This book contains actual X-rays that Jessica gets to view as she takes a tour of the hospital after her arm is broken.

EXPANSION:

Obtain discarded X-rays from a doctor's office. Names may be cut off the film to ensure patient confidentiality. During role-play, the technician may share the X-rays with the patient.

Yemen's Fruit

DISCUSSION SUGGESTIONS:

✄ Yemen is a country in the Middle East that has green valleys and mountains.

✄ Fruit and bread are staple foods in Yemen.

✄ Yemen's fruit crops include apricots, bananas, grapes, and mangoes.

✄ Yemenis do not eat their meals at a table. They sit on the floor. The food is arranged in pots and dishes on a colorful plastic cloth.

✄ They do not use silverware in Yemen. Food is scooped up with bread or the right hand. The left hand is never used to eat with, as it is the hand that cleans the body after toileting.

✄ Food is not put on a plate. Everyone eats from the dishes closest to them.

✄ If you are a visitor in Yemen, to refuse food would insult the host. If you refuse food, it means you think the host cannot afford to feed you, or you think the food is not clean, or you do not like the host (Hestler, 1999).

ADULT PREPARATION:

1. Wash hands.
2. Wash the apricots, grapes, and mangoes.

PROCEDURES:

The child will complete the following steps:

1. Find the state he or she lives in on the globe with the adult's assistance.
2. Find Yemen on the globe with the adult's assistance. Note the distance between the two.
3. Wash hands.
4. Identify the apricots, bananas, grapes, and mangoes.
5. Watch the adult cut the apricots, bananas, grapes, and mangoes and place them in separate bowls.
6. Place 1–2 spoonfuls of each fruit into a bowl.
7. Identify which hand is the right hand.
8. Eat fruit with the right hand.

continued

131

AGES: 3–5

GROUP SIZE:
3–4 children

DEVELOPMENTAL GOALS:

✄ To recognize fruit grown in another country

✄ To create a healthy snack

LEARNING OBJECTIVE:

Using a globe, fruit, a bowl, and spoons, the child will create a nutrition snack with produce.

MATERIALS:

Knife
Cutting board
Apricots
Bananas
Grapes
Mangoes
Bowls
Globe
Spoons

Yemen's Fruit continued

① SAFETY PRECAUTIONS:

✂ Supervise children closely when eating small pieces of food, to prevent chocking.

✂ Always check for food allergies before beginning a cooking project.

Yo-Yo: An International Toy

DISCUSSION SUGGESTIONS:

✄ The yo-yo has been an international toy.

✄ It is thought to have originated in China. However, the first mention of the yo-yo was in 500 B.C. in Greece.

✄ It was used in 16th-century Philippines.

✄ It has been documented in 18th-century India, France, and England. The yo-yo became very popular in 20th-century United States.

✄ In 1962, the Duncan Company sold 45 million yo-yos in the United States. This was at a time when there were only 40 million children in the nation (American Yo-Yo Association Newsletter, 1997).

continued

AGES: 3–5

GROUP SIZE:
4–10 children

DEVELOPMENTAL GOALS:

✄ To find similarities among cultures

✄ To stimulate eye-hand coordination

LEARNING OBJECTIVE:

Using plastic yo-yos, globe, adding machine tape, markers, stapler, staples, straw, and a rubber band, the children will create and play with yo-yos.

MATERIALS:

Adding machine tape
Scissors
Plastic yo-yos
Basket
Globe
Markers
Stapler and staples
Plastic straws
Rubber bands

Yo-Yo: An International Toy continued

ADULT PREPARATION:

1. Cut off one 2'–3' section of adding machine tape for each child.
2. Put one yo-yo for each child in a basket.

PROCEDURES:

The children will complete the following steps:

1. Sit in a circle or semicircle.
2. Take turns finding various places on the globe where the yo-yo has been popular (i.e., China, Greece, Philippines, France, England, and the United States). Use adult assistance if necessary.
3. Select a yo-yo out of the basket.
4. Attempt to make the yo-yo run up and down the string.
5. Put the yo-yos back in the basket and then sit at a table.
6. Begin to make an individual Chinese yo-yo by using markers to color a design on the 2–3 foot section of adding machine tape.
7. Write their name on their design, with adult assistance if necessary.

The adult will complete the following steps:

1. Staple the end of the adding machine tape to the end of a straw at a 90-degree angle to the straw.
2. Roll the paper tightly around the straw and fasten with a rubber band.
3. Allow the paper to set overnight.
4. The next day, take the rubber band off and give to children to use like a Chinese yo-yo. Hold the yo-yo with one hand. Children flick their wrist, throwing the yo-yo straight out.

NOTES:

✂ Yo-yos with a plastic string will have a better outcome for young children.

✂ Chinese yo-yos may be purchased from party supply stores.

Zambian *Nshima*

DISCUSSION SUGGESTIONS:

✂ *Nshima* (in-shee-mah) is a staple food eaten by Zambians.

✂ It is made from ground corn and water and is the consistency of a firm porridge (Holmes, 1998).

✂ It is generally eaten for lunch and dinner and is served with a vegetable, legume, meat, or fish (Tembo, n.d.).

ADULT PREPARATION:

1. Set the electric skillet on the table. Plug it into an outlet. Tape the electric cord to the table and floor, so no one will accidentally pull the appliance by the cord.
2. Roll towels and place them around the skillet to prevent burning.
3. Wash hands.
4. Measure 1 cup of warm water into the electric skillet.
5. Measure ½ cup of cornmeal and pour it into a bowl.
6. Turn the skillet onto medium heat.

PROCEDURES:

The children will complete the following steps:

1. Find the state he or she lives in on the globe with the adult's assistance.
2. Find Zambia on the globe with the adult's assistance. Note the distance between the two.
3. Wash hands.
4. Take turns to:
   a. Measure 1 tablespoon of cornmeal.
   b. Put the cornmeal in the water.
   c. Stir the mixture with the long-handled wooden spoon.
5. Continue step 4 until all the cornmeal has been added.

The adult will complete the following steps:

1. Continue to stir the *nshima* until it comes to a boil.
2. Remove the skillet from the children's reach, turn the heat to low and simmer for approximately 15 minutes or until the *nshima* rolls into a ball.

continued

AGES: 3–5

GROUP SIZE:
2–3 children

DEVELOPMENTAL GOALS:

✂ To experience food from another culture

✂ To develop global connections

LEARNING OBJECTIVE:

Using an electric skillet, warm water, cornmeal, tablespoon, long-handled wooden spoon, towels, and tape, the children will work together to make *nshima*.

MATERIALS:

Electric skillet
Masking tape
Towels
Measuring cup
Warm water
Cornmeal
Bowl
Tablespoon
Long-handled wooden spoon
Plates
Optional: vegetables, beans, or meat

Zambian Nshima continued

3. Allow the *nshima* to cool.

4. Divide the *nshima* onto plates and serve at snack time. The children pinch pieces off and eat it with their fingers. It may be eaten with vegetables, beans, or meat.

SAFETY PRECAUTIONS:

✄ Supervise children constantly when using a hot appliance. Check with your center's policies regarding cooking in the classroom. If cooking is not allowed in the classroom, mix all ingredients in a saucepan in the room, then cook the *nshima* in the kitchen.

✄ Check for food allergies before beginning a cooking activity.

Zookeeper

AGES: 3–5

GROUP SIZE:

2–3 children

DEVELOPMENTAL GOALS:

- ✂ To develop respect for different occupations
- ✂ To stimulate classification skills

LEARNING OBJECTIVE:

Using blocks, stuffed animals, and bowls, the child will take care of the zoo animals.

MATERIALS:

Marker
Construction paper
Masking tape
Stuffed animals
Bowls
Blocks
Book about zookeeper
Large sheet of paper

DISCUSSION SUGGESTIONS:

- ✂ A zookeeper takes care of animals and keeps their habitats clean.
- ✂ A habitat is the environment where the animals live.
- ✂ Zookeepers try to keep the animal's habitat close to what it would be if the animal were in the wild.
- ✂ To take care of the animals, a zookeeper feeds them and may wash or bathe them.

ADULT PREPARATION:

1. Write *Zookeeper* on a piece of construction paper.
2. Tape the sign to the wall.
3. Place the animals and bowls in the block center.

PROCEDURES:

The child will complete the following steps:

1. Listen to book read about zookeepers.
2. Answer the adult's question, "What do zookeepers do?"

continued

Zookeeper continued

3. Watch adult write response on a large sheet of paper.
4. Sort the animals by type (i.e., all monkeys together, all bears together).
5. Build habitats for each type of animal with blocks.
6. Put the animals in their habitats.
7. Put bowls in the habitats to pretend to feed the animals.

⚠ SAFETY PRECAUTION:

Watch children closely when using small objects, to prevent choking hazards.

NOTE:

Pieces of play dough or foam packing peanuts may be used for food. Check with your school to see if foam packing peanuts are allowed.

BOOK SUGGESTION:

We Need Zookeepers by Lisa Trumbauer (Mankato, MN: Capstone Press, 2003). The different duties of a zookeeper are explored in this easy book. A one-word sentence accompanies each colorful photograph.

References

2006 White House Easter egg roll. (2006). *The White House.* Retrieved June 28, 2006, from http://www.whitehouse.gov/easter/2006

Ackerman, K. (1988). *Song and dance man.* New York: Alfred A. Knopf.

Adamson, H. (2004). *A day in the life of a farmer.* Mankato, MN: Capstone Press.

Adamson, H. (2004). *A day in the life of a police officer.* Mankato, MN: Capstone Press.

Amazing animals of the world. (1995). Danbury, CT: Grolier Educational Corporation.

American Yo-Yo Association Newsletter. (September 1997). Spanaway, WA.

Amos, J. (2002). *Being kind.* Milwaukee, WI: Gareth Stevens Publishing.

Anderson, C. (2005). *Bread bakery.* Chicago, IL: Heinemann Library.

Arbor day. (2005). TreeHelp.com. Retrieved January 2, 2006, from http://www.arbor-day.net/arbor-day-state-dates.htm

Augustin, B. & Augustin, R.A. (1997). *Qatar.* New York: Children's Press.

Azarian, M. (2000). *A gardener's alphabet.* Boston, MA: Houghton Mifflin Company.

Blackstone, S. (2002). *An Island in the Sun.* Cambridge, MA: Barefoot Books.

Bonney, B. (1997). *Soccer: Skills.* Vero Beach, FL: The Rourke Press, Inc.

Bourgeois, P. (1991). *Franklin fibs.* New York: Scholastic, Inc.

Bourgeois, P. (1999). *Postal workers.* Buffalo, NY: Kids Can Press.

Bowen, R. A., (2003). *The Native Americans.* Philadelphia, PA: Mason Crest Publishers.

Britton, T. L. (2004). *Denmark.* Edina, MN: Abdo Publishing Company.

Butler, J. (2001). *Pi-shu, the little panda.* Atlanta, GA: Peachtree Publishers.

Carle, E. (1995) *Walter the baker.* New York: Simon & Schuster Books for Young Readers.

Catala, E. (2004). *What does a firefighter do?* Mankato, MN: Capstone Press.

Chalmers, M. (1981). *Come to the doctor, Harry.* New York: Harper Collins Children's Books.

Chocolate, D. M. N. (1992). *My first Kwanzaa book.* New York: Scholastic, Inc.

Christelow, E. (2003). *Vote!* New York: Clarion Books.

Cousins, L. (2000). *Maisy drives the bus.* Cambridge, MA: Candlewick Press.

Crewe, S. (1996). *Maps and globes.* New York: Children's Press.

de Regniers, B. (1964). *May I bring a friend?* New York: Atheneum.

Devlin, W. (1999). History of the piñata. *Mexico Connect.* Retrieved June 27, 2006, from http://www.mexconnect.com/mex_/travel/wdevlin/wdpinatahistory.html

Douglas, L. G., (2003). *The Liberty Bell.* New York: Rosen Book Works, Inc.

Everything you need to know about ice fishing. (n.d.). Retrieved June 16, 2006, from Wisconson Department of Natural Resources' Environmental Education for Kids (EEK!) Web site: http://www.dnr.state.wi.us/org/caer/ce/eek/nature/icefish.htm#ice

Enchanted learning. (2006). *Rainforest animals.* Retrieved June 28, 2006, from http://www.enchantedlearning.com/subjects/rainforest

Feldman, G. C., & Gradwohl, J. (n.d.) Ocean currents. *Ocean Planet.* Retrieved June 14, 2006, from http://seawifs.gsfc.nasa.gov/OCEAN_PLANET/HTML/oceanography_currents_1.html

Fluet, C. (2005). *A day in the life of a nurse.* Mankato, MN: Capstone Press.

Fox, C., & Fox, D. (2001). *Fire fighter Piggy Wiggy.* Brooklyn, NY: Handprint Books.

Frost, H. (1999). *Going to the dentist.* Mankato, MN: Capstone Press.

Frost, H. (2002). *Independence Day.* Mankato, MN: Capstone Press.

Gibbons, G. (1999). *Exploring the deep, dark sea.* New York: Little, Brown and Company.

Hennessy, B.G. (1996). *Olympics!* New York: Penguin Group.

Hestler, A. (1999). *Yemen.* New York: Marshall Cavendish Corporation.

Hestler, A. (2001). *Wales.* New York: Marshall Cavendish Corporation.

Hise, P. (2004, April). Orange alert: Protect yourself from foodborne illness. *Vegetarian Times, 320,* 79–83.

The history of Arbor Day (n.d.) *The National Arbor Day Foundation.* Retrieved May 29, 2006, from http://www.arborday.org/arborday/history.cfm

History of the Easter egg roll. Retrieved December 10, 2005, from www.whitehouse.gov/easter/history.html

Hoena, B. A. (2005). *Weather ABC.* Mankato, MN: Capstone Press.

Holmes, T. (1998). *Zambia.* New York: Marshall Cavendish Corporation.

Hopkins, L. B. (2004). *Hanukkah lights.* New York: HarperCollins Publishers, Inc.

Hughes, M. (2004). *My first visit to the dentist.* Chicago: Raintree.

Jaques, F. P. (2003). *There once was a puffin.* New York: North-South Books.

Jordan, M. A. (1996) *Good cook's book of tomatoes.* Retrieved June 27, 2006, from http://www.globalgourmet.com/food/egg/egg0896/gazpacho.html

Kachenmeista, C. (1989). *On Monday when it rained.* New York: Houghton Mifflin Company.

King, D. C. (1998). *Colonial days.* New York: John Wiley & Sons, Inc.

Kleven, E. (1996). *Hooray! A piñata!* New York: Dutton Children's Books.

LaFosse, M. G. (2002). *Making origami fish step by step.* New York: PowerKids Press.

Leeper, A. (2005). *I am honest.* Chicago: Heinemann Library.

The lei tradition. (2005). *Hawaiian Flower Lei.* Retrieved June 27, 2006, from http://www.hawaiiflowerlei.com/leitradition.asp

Liberty Bell Museum. (2006). *FAQs about the Liberty Bell.* Retrieved June 28, 2006, from http://www.libertybellmuseum.com/faqs.htm

Marshall, J. (1989). *The three little pigs*. New York: Dial Books for Young Readers.

McPhail, D. (1984). *Fix-it*. New York: E.P. Dutton.

Middleton, H. (2003). *Modern Olympics*. Chicago: Heinemann Library.

Moncure, J. (1997). *The child's world of kindness*. Chanhassen, MN: Child's World, Inc.

Morris, A. (1992). *Houses and homes*. New York: Lothrop, Lee & Shepard Books.

Morris, A. (2000). *Families*. New York: HarperCollins Publishers.

Murrell, K. B. (1998). *Russia*. New York: Dorling Kindersley Publishing, Inc.

Mitchell, M. (2004). *Stars*. Minneapolis, MN: Lerner Publications Company.

Nicolei, M. (1998). *Kitaq*. Anchorage, AK: Alaska Northwest Books.

Parish, S. (2003). *Australian wildlife*. Philadelphia, PA: Mason Crest Publishers.

People at work (2005). Indianapolis, IN: JIST Publishing, Inc.

Putnam, J. (2004). *Eyewitness pyramid*. New York: Dorling Kindersley Publishing, Inc.

Risso, J. (2001). Venezuelans love arepas! *TOPICS online Magazine*. Retrieved June 27, 2006, from http://www.topics-mag.com/edition7/arepas.htm

Ross, P. (1999). *The Pueblo Indians*. Mankato, MN: Bridgestone Books.

Rylant, C. (1985). *The relatives came*. New York: Bradbury Press.

Saffer, B. (2002). *Kenya*. Mankato, MN: Capstone Press.

Sakurai, G. (1996). *The Liberty Bell*. New York: Children's Press.

Salas, L. P. (2006). *Whose shoes are these?* Minneapolis, MN: Picture Window Books.

Saunders-Smith, G. (2000). *We need farmers*. Mankato, MN: Pebble Books.

Say, A. (1993). *Grandfather's journey*. Boston, MA: Houghton Mifflin Company.

Seeger, L.V. (2005). *Walter was worried*. New Milford, CT: Roaring Brook Press.

Seeger, P. (1994). *Abiyoyo*. New York: Simon & Schuster.

Sirimarco, E. (2000). *At the bank*. San Juan Capistrano, CA: The Child's World.

Spinelli, E. (2000). *Night shift daddy*. New York: Hyperion Books for Children.

Stille, D. (1997). *Trucks*. New York: Children's Press.

Tembo, M. S. (n.d.) *Nshima Zambian staple food*. Retrieved January 3, 2006, from http://www.bridgewater.edu/~mtembo/nshimachapter1.htm

Thaler, M. (2001). *The custodian from the black lagoon*. New York: Scholastic, Inc.

Trumbauer, L. (2002). *What are oceans?* Mankato, MN: Capstone Press.

Trumbauer, L. (2003). *We need zoo keepers*. Mankato, MN: Capstone Press.

University of Delaware. (n.d.) *Test your ocean IQ*. Retrieved June 14, 2006, from http://www.ocean.udel.edu/deepsea/questions/question.html

Vantage Adventures. (2004). *Antwerp*. Retrieved May 24, 2006, from http://www.travelvantage.com/antwerp.html

Webster's dictionary and Roget's thesaurus. (2001). Weston, FL: Paradise Press, Inc.

Wikipedia. (15 April 2006). *Greek pizza*. Retrieved June 28, 2006, from http://en.wikipedia.org/wiki/Greek_pizza

Ziefert, H. (1995). *The three little pigs*. New York: Viking.

Appendix A

AUSTRALIA'S ANIMALS (A1–A8)

A1. AUSTRALIAN CROCODILE

A2. AUSTRALIAN SPINY ANTEATER

A3. BANDICOOT

A4. DINGO

A5. EMU

A6. KANGAROO

A8. KOOKABURRA

A9. DEPOSIT SLIP

⭐ **ABC BANK**

ABC BANK LIMITED
BANK STREET LANE

Deposit Slip

Paid in by _____

Credit account of

" 123456: 003754100101 " 50

Date _____

Notes _____

Coin _____

Checks _____
per back

$

AIO. CHINESE PANDA BEAR

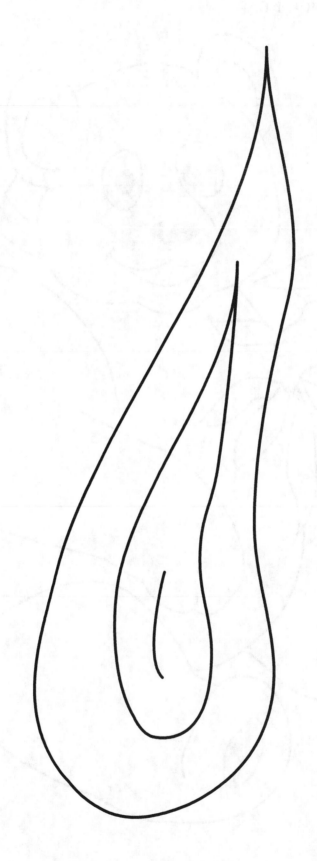

A12. PYRAMID

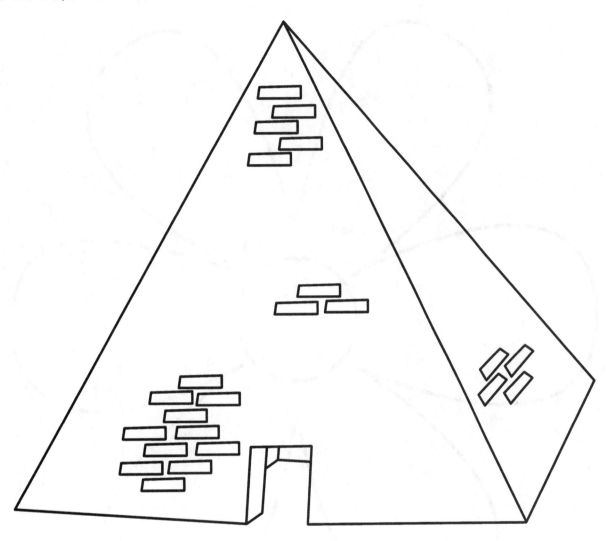

A13. FLOWER

A14. FISH

JUNGLE ANIMALS (A15-A19)

A15. FROG

A16. GREEN IGUANA

A17. MANDRILL MONKEY

A18. SNAKE

A19. TOUCAN

A20. JUNGLE ANIMAL TALLY SHEET

KINDNESS PATTERNS (A21–A24)

A21. CHILD HOLDING DOOR OPEN FOR ANOTHER

A22. CHILD SHARING TOYS WITH ANOTHER

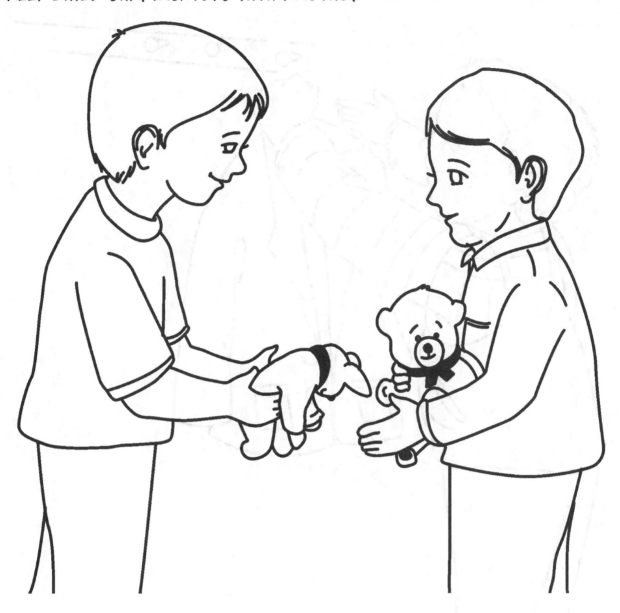

A23. CHILD HANGING UP HIS COAT

A24. CHILD GIVING ANOTHER CHILD A HUG

A25. LIBERTY BELL

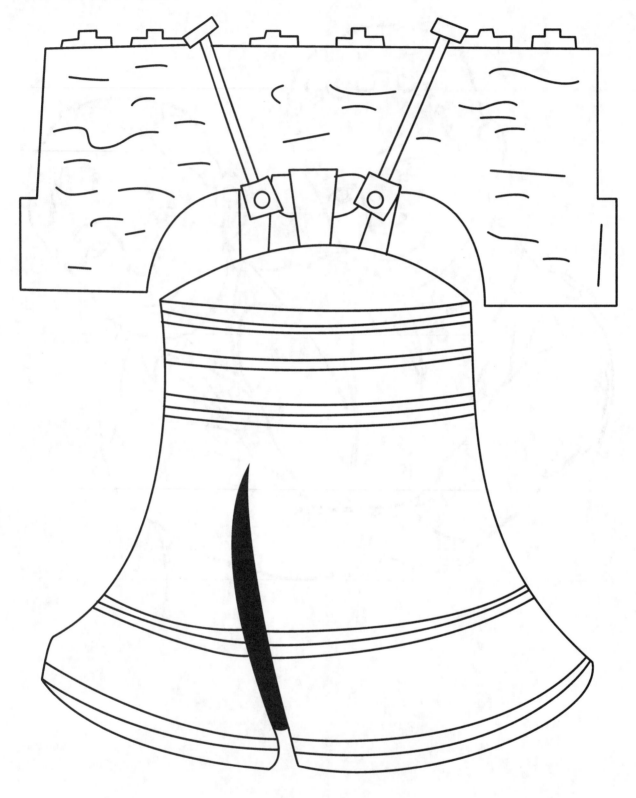

A26. WOODEN SHOE

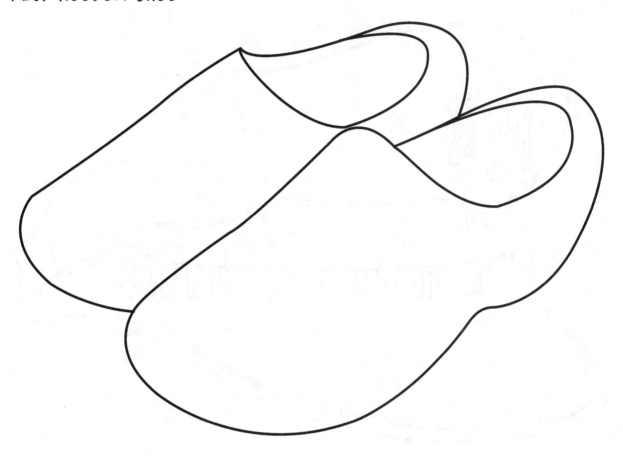

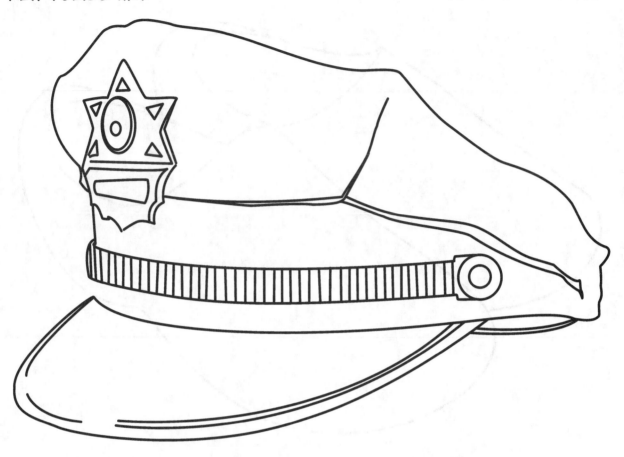

A28. CAMEL HEAD

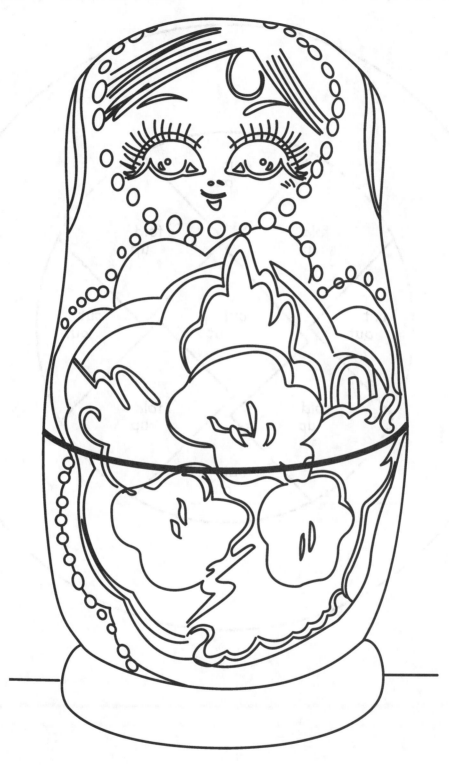

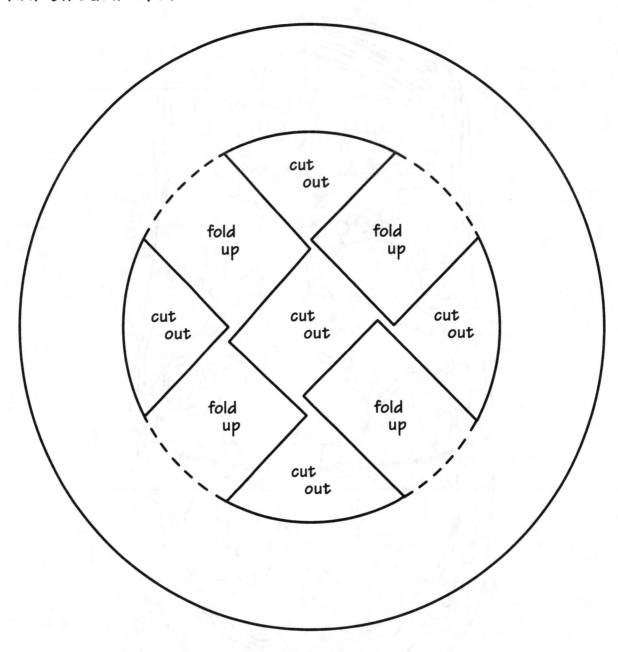

A32. BIRTHDAY CAKE

UNIFORM PATTERNS (A33-A36)

A33. POLICE OFFICER

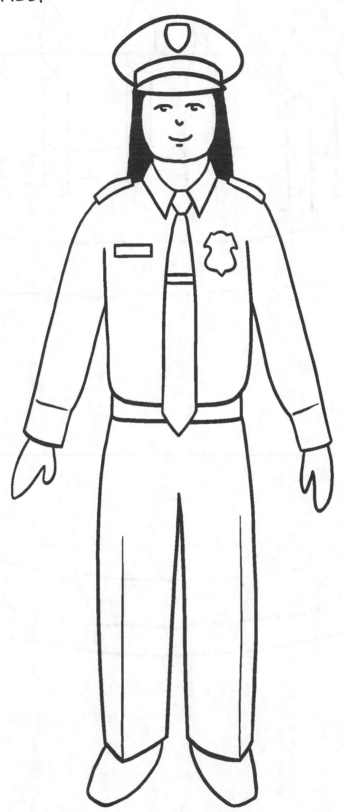

A34. MAIL CARRIER

PICTURES OF PEOPLE AT WORK IN THEIR UNIFORMS (A37-A40)

A37. POLICE OFFICER AT POLICE STATION

A39. DOCTOR IN THE OFFICE WITH A PATIENT

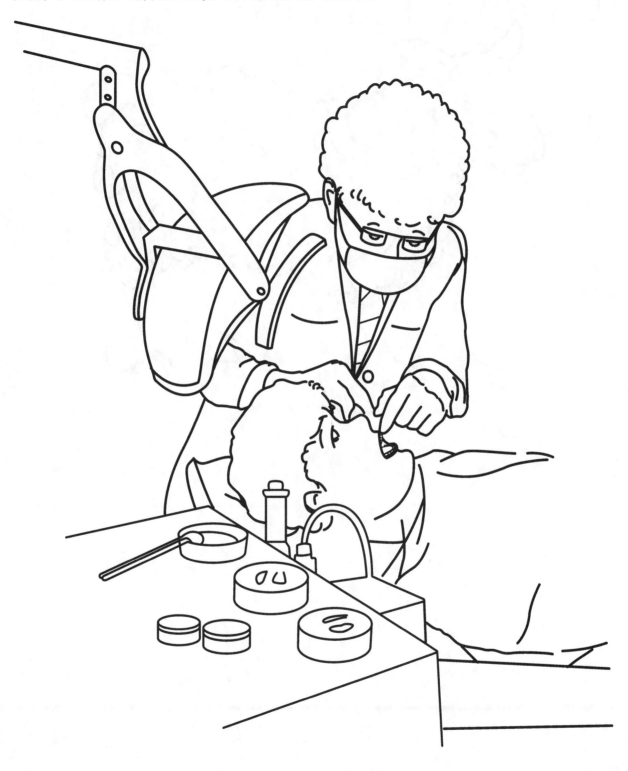

A4l. SHEEP

WEATHER SYMBOLS (A42–A45)

A42. UMBRELLA

A43. SUN

A44. CLOUD

A45. SNOWFLAKE

Appendix B

B1. Family Letter 1

Date:

Dear Family,

We are discussing our families in class and are creating a class family book.

Please send in a picture of _____'s family by

_____.

On the back of the picture, please write the family members' names and their relationship to your child. We will not be able to return the pictures.

Sincerely,

B2. Permission form to be photographed and videotaped

My child, _____ has permission to be photographed or videotaped for educational purposes and/or class activities while attending _____ (Child care center or school).

Parent's signature _____

Date_____

B3. Family Letter 2

Date:

Dear Family,

We are studying grandparents. Please send in a stamped addressed envelope with your child's grandparent's address by _____.
You may send in more than one envelope for your child to "write" to more than one grandparent.
If your child does not have a grandparent to write to, we will send letters to a nearby nursing home.

Sincerely,

B4. Family Letter 3

Date:

Dear Family,

We are studying homes. Will you please send in a picture of your house, apartment building, duplex, etc? Please send it in with your child by _____.

Sincerely,

B5. Family Letter 4

Date:

Dear Family,

We are preserving part of your child's personal history. Please send in a shoe that your child has outgrown by _____.

Sincerely,

B6. Family Letter 5

Date:

Dear Family,

We are studying where our family members live across the continental United States. Please write the family member, state he or she lives in, and relationship to your child below and return by

_____.

Sincerely,

Appendix C

Curriculum Index

Index